Nightmare Culture

ALEX DE JONGE

Nightmare Culture

Lautréamont and *Les Chants de Maldoror*

St. Martin's Press · New York

Affiliated Publishers: Macmillan Limited, London
—also at Bombay, Calcutta, Madras and Melbourne

. . . a constant tension between 'culture' and 'life'. For it is the necessary destiny of culture that everything which it creates in its constituent process of *Bildung* removes us more and more from the originality of life. The more richly and energetically the human spirit engages its formative activity the further this very activity seems to remove it from the primal source of its own being. More and more, it appears to be imprisoned in its own creations, in the words of language, in the image of myth and art, in the intellectual symbols of cognition, which cover it like a delicate and transparent but unbreakable veil ... If all Culture is manifested in the creation of a specific image-world, of specific symbolic forms, the aim of philosophy is not to go beyond all these creations, but rather to understand and elucidate their basic formative principle. It is solely through the awareness of this principle that the content of life acquires its true form.

E. Cassirer, *The Philosophy of Symbolic Forms*

CONTENTS

Introduction to Nightmare

Lautréamont begins his principal work *Les Chants de Maldoror* with a warning; unless the reader proceeds with real caution Lautréamont's poetry will poison his brain. This may appear a hysterical and exaggerated threat, but it is nothing of the sort, the author is perfectly right. Read in one way the work will make the reader aware of appetites and desires that he never knew he had; he may not like what he finds, or he may like it too much. Reading in another way he will discover that Lautréamont delicately picks at the threads that hold his world-view together until, gently and undramatically, its fabric falls apart at the seams. But however he may choose to interpret or judge *Les Chants de Maldoror,* he may be certain of one thing; it is a work that does not leave the reader as it found him.

Lautréamont forces his readers to stop taking their world for granted. He shatters the complacent acceptance of the reality proposed by their cultural traditions, and makes them see that reality for what it is: an unreal nightmare all the more hair-raising because the sleeper believes that he is awake.

The desire to bring his readers to full consciousness, make them see who and where they are, underlies every word that Lautréamont wrote. Above all he wants us to understand that we are prisoners confined for ever in the nightmare of our culture. He is traumatically disturbed by the knowledge that we can only see the world as our culture would have us see it; that our view of reality is strictly the limited view that you enjoy from a cell window.

In order to make us acknowledge this truth emotionally as well as intellectually, Lautréamont sets out to disturb us. Coolly, deliberately, he breaks every kind of taboo. His blasphemies are so extreme that they continue to disturb in an age of irreligion; his sadistic eroticism has lost none of its edge in a world no longer shocked by death camps and hard porn.

Lautréamont is not, however, content simply to shock his

1

readers. He also asks them questions, questions such as 'What is literature?' 'What is meaning?' 'What is man?' And, finally, 'What is God?' Although he supplies no answers he makes us realise that the questions need to be asked, because the obvious answer answers nothing. Thus Lautréamont seeks to heighten awareness in his readers, to teach them to think and feel for themselves.

His instrument of education is language. With an extraordinary blend of surrealism and logic he uses language as a model to build patterns that clarify and articulate the issues at stake. The models are not designed to provide answers, but to *explicate* the questions, taking that word in its etymological sense of *explicare*—to unfold.

It is this process of unfolding that makes Lautréamont important. He is not just another minor poet, a rich and untapped vein of scholarship material, to be written about because he is there. If we read him with both eyes open, we shall see that his poetry unfolds before us the essential elements of our culture-pattern – post-Renaissance capitalist Europeans with a Christian ancestry.

The most important lesson that his models teach is that man is at the mercy of his culture-pattern. Culture creates for each one of us a 'grid'; a set of categories of similarity and difference that forms the entire series of values and beliefs through which we interpret our world. It is a great deal harder to change the grid than it is to be changed by it, because it constitutes the base-elements of a cultural language. It is an enormous mistake to assume that language is something we manipulate; usually it is language that manipulates us. Since it is a collective phenomenon, the product of a tacit consensus on the part of the group, each individual is at the mercy of his language. He may feel that it leaves him free to do as he pleases, but that sense of freedom is an illusion. He is always restricted by the range of choices that language offers him. He can only criticise it in terms of its own making. It creates for him a prison from which there can be no escape. As Wilhelm von Humboldt writes,

Man lives with his objects chiefly—in fact, since his feeling and acting depend on his perceptions, one might say exclusively—as language presents them to him. By the same process whereby he spins language out of his own being, he ensnares himself in it: and each language draws a magic circle around the people to whom it belongs, a circle from which there is no escape save by stepping out of it into another.[1]

In other words, language creates what might be termed a one-dimensional situation; one in which it is impossible to make an act of effective judgment, because the very situation renders us quite unable to conceive of any genuine alternative. The individual is not free to give his own answer, because no answer he gives can be his own.

Lautréamont is obsessed with the fact that our answers are not our own, but simply the products of our culture, of our particular place in space and time. What we think of as being our truth is nothing of the sort; it is imposed upon us by circumstance, making us at the very least the prisoners of our culture.

Lautréamont cannot secure our release. As von Humboldt implied, you cannot escape from this prison, you can only change cells. What he can do is make us realise that we are 'inside', show us the walls, the bars on the window, and perhaps, something beyond. This is the next best thing to escape; once we know where we are, and realise that all action and judgment is shaped by our situation, we experience a strange liberation. The better we know our prison, the larger our cell seems to become. Not even Lautréamont can arrange a break-out, but he can make prison-life more bearable.

It is to this end that Lautréamont blasts his readers with blasphemy and obscenity. He tries to break down their prejudices, the inhibitions founded on good taste and taboo that culture builds into them as a defence against any truth that might threaten it. He goes on to try to make them understand the actual nature of their predicament. It is precisely because his work considers these fundamental questions, questions that pose an essential threat to the culture-pattern in that they seek to expose its limitations, that the immediate response of the culture in question is to reject Lautréamont as unreadable.

There are certain fundamentally subversive works that official culture cannot afford to acknowledge. They offer too great a threat, because they infringe the area of silence surrounding society's basic taboos. We all know the proposition 'Tell me what you read and I'll tell you who you are'. Much more revealing is the proposition 'Tell me what you censor and I'll tell you who you are'. Some of the most significant facts about a society are to be found in its cultural dustbins, among the objects that it rejects because they do not conform to its patterns.

Official culture subscribes to the Berkeleyan thesis, whereby an author exists only in so far as the public is aware of him. It has endeavoured to make Lautréamont vanish by pretending he is not really there. He does not loom large in the official canon of nineteenth-century European poetry. It was significantly left to the surrealists of the 1920s to recognise him as a writer of the utmost importance. Their admiration for him was boundless—no wonder. Surrealism represents one of the most radical rejections of official culture that we know. The surrealists considered that their civilisation had most perfectly expressed itself in such masterpieces as the Battle of the Somme. They found it more difficult to admire its lesser creations. For them *Les Chants de Maldoror* expressed a refusal to accept the rationalistic commonsense world-view that formed the basis of that civilisation. They felt it was a work that the establishment could not afford to face; a work to be taken very seriously indeed.

Not so official criticism. Because the author challenges basic assumptions and declines to accept cultural conventions as the truth, his writing is quite unlike anything else in the cultural tradition. It cannot be matched against a predecessor, it lacks 'formative influences'. Because it demands a totally new way of reading, official criticism dismisses it as impossible to read.

But even if Lautréamont were easy to read, he would still be rejected out of hand. The work is easier to explain away than to accept. So great is the violence it inflicts that it inspires immediate resentment. It is simpler to dismiss it.

The dismissal of a work that is too challenging for comfort expresses itself with the excessive protestation of a concealed gut-reaction. The work may be rejected as formless—because the form is not a traditional one. If the work is strong enough to reach its audience despite its lack of form, other defences are brought into play. Its rhetoric may be admired, grudgingly. It

4

is conceded that Lautréamont created some brilliant images but that these are swamped in turgid extravagance. Léon Bloy describes the form of *Les Chants de Maldoror* as 'liquid lava'. Alternatively the work may be dismissed as a youthful indiscretion. It is alleged to reflect an immature personality, prone to paranoid histrionics; therefore it is not to be taken seriously. That this argument also 'takes out' Rimbaud and Rousseau cannot be helped; a certain amount of critical overkill is inevitable.

Official criticism finds it convenient to treat *Les Chants de Maldoror* as a curiosity, an exhibit in the literary freak-show. This enables it to dismiss its hair-raising obscenity as schoolboy extravagance. The patronising treatment of the author as a foul-mouthed innocent enables the critic to dodge the violent eroticism of his work. He does not have to take account of scenes in which innocent children are raped to death with the aid of a pen-knife and a bulldog, in which God is caught in an informal moment resting in a whore's crib. Such scenes are mere adolescent indiscretions, they do not matter, are not really there. This kind of dismissal has been used to take care of writers such as Céline, not *really* anti-Semitic, and William Burroughs, not a real writer, since he enjoys the support of a fortune built on the sale of office machinery. The alternative—to accept the works as meaning what they say—would be unthinkable.

But Lautréamont is precisely concerned with the unthinkable. Hence the deliberate flouting of taboo, the persistent intention to name the unnameable that emerges in such passages as this:

> It is time to apply a brake to my inspiration and to pause for a moment on my way, as you do when you look at a woman's vagina.[2]

What is to be done with an author, a nineteenth-century author at that, who uses *that word*? The answer is obvious. He must be hidden. You either pretend he does not exist, or you put him away. You do not, on any account, read him.

It is no coincidence that a great predecessor of Lautréamont's, one of the most prolific novelists of the eighteenth century, has been subjected to just such a conspiracy of silence and sequestration. The Marquis de Sade spent most of his adult life behind bars, and his writing has been kept in the quarantine of the pornographers' lists ever since. It would be unthinkable to treat de Sade as literature; to read him with both hands. This is why the case against him is always made out on literary grounds. We are informed that his works are formless, repetitive, boring, that they are not even erotic. He is both a bad writer and a bad pornographer. Official criticism labels him unreadable, so no one tries.

Just as de Sade has been dismissed as a repetitive lunatic, so there have been attempts to explain Lautréamont by suggesting that he was mad. Known to be the work of a madman, the writing is no longer a threat. It ceases to have meaning and becomes a curiosity: a text with a clinical or documentary value. Thus one critic, a certain Soulier, 'proves' that Lautréamont suffered from schizophrenia. Similar arguments have been applied to Artaud's *Theatre of Cruelty*. The fact that its author spent his later years in an asylum invalidates his work.

A much more convincing dismissal of Lautréamont is furnished by the 'near-miss' approach, whereby *Les Chants de Maldoror* just fails. Albert Camus has described it as the work of 'a schoolboy who was nearly a genius'. This constitutes the most generous and damning of rejection slips. 'Very well done. This was extremely interesting. Do carry on and send us anything you do when you're grown up.' It is a little odd to find Camus writing like this about a work that anticipates his own interest in the cultural outsider by more than half a century.

This brief review of the critical reaction to Lautréamont tells us more about the critics than it does about the object of their criticism. Reading Lautréamont and reflecting about what he has to say will often lead one into areas of speculation that may have little to do with French poetry in the last century, but that have a great deal to do with the way we live and think now. Since he writes about the relationship between the individual and his culture, he can perform the invaluable service of helping us discover who and where we are.

It is because the work is not a conventional piece of literature that we shall find ourselves paying less than customary attention to conventional literary values. Little will be said about the life and times of the author. This is partly because very little is known about his life, principally because he goes to extreme lengths to make his readers understand that his writing is in no sense autobiographical or confessional. Although there will be no paraphrase of the work as such, the reader who has read no Lautréamont, or indeed who reads no French, will be at no disadvantage. It is for such a reader that this work is primarily intended. If the 'innocent' reader can be prevailed upon to persevere, he will get the feel of Lautréamont's writing, will grow familiar with his principal themes, will have read a number of his work's key episodes, and will acquire a sense of the relationship that it bears to his own experience, a relationship that exists regardless of any interest in French poetry of the last century.

But before entering the world of Maldoror the reader should beware. At its strongest Lautréamont's strange blend of bombast, blasphemy and obscenity is very disturbing. It will be recalled that the author began his work with a warning. With its invocation, its absurdly complicated style and its bizarre imagery, it is an excellent introduction to Lautréamont's nightmare:

> Please heaven that the reader, rendered for a moment bold and savage at what he reads, find his rough and wild path, without getting lost, across the desolate marshes of these sombre poison-ridden pages; for unless his reading be supported by a rigorous logic and a mental alertness at least the equal of his sense of mistrust, the deadly vapours of this book will saturate his soul as water saturates sugar.[3]

The reader has been warned.

PART ONE

Isidore Ducasse : Le Comte de Lautréamont : Maldoror

CHAPTER ONE

In Place of a Biography

From the very outset it can be seen that Lautréamont's work makes a break with the received idea of literature. The author of *Les Chants de Maldoror* does not sign his own name to his creation; he hides behind a pseudonym. Indeed the casual reader may not be at all sure who the author really is. Is he the Comte de Lautréamont? The name is an unfamiliar one, it does not feature in the Almanach de Gotha. Literary histories inform us that the real author was a certain Isidore Ducasse, a young Frenchman from Montevideo who took Lautréamont as his *nom de plume*. But perhaps both these names are masks that conceal behind them the sinister figure of the true author: the murderer and rapist Maldoror? The text leaves the question open. Its very title, '*Les Chants de Maldoror* par le Comte de Lautréamont', is a contradiction in terms. If Lautréamont wrote them, why are they Maldoror's *Chants*? The vexing problem of identity is compounded by the way in which the work is written. It moves freely from first to third person singular in mid-paragraph. The distinction between 'I' and 'He' is made meaningless.

Even if we make the prosaic choice and assume that the book was the work of Ducasse, our problems are not over. Despite the valiant efforts of his biographers, Ducasse is one of those rare figures of Western culture, a writer without a biography.

Biography is of course one of the mainstays of our critical tradition. If you find it difficult to discuss Rimbaud's poetry, find out what he did in Abyssinia. We all know the approach that seeks the author through his writing, uses his words as a way through the looking-glass to discover, on the other side, the ambiguous figure of the man himself. Racine, Voltaire or Stendhal are present in their works, and yet suitably absent. Their self-portraits are inferred, not stated, and hence are pleasingly incomplete.

The biographical approach, that seeks to recreate an identikit portrait of an author from the fragmented self-portrayals of his works, can be very useful. Authors do tend to portray themselves in their work, and it is not uninteresting to discover just who they were. Biography can illuminate the work, at one remove, by placing it in a context. Moreover authors, like saints and royalty, often have interesting and eventful lives, and there is no reason why scholars should not devote themselves to this particular branch of secular hagiography. What can be done for Mary Queen of Scots can be equally well done for Prosper Mérimée, and the public has a right to know the identity of Proust's boyfriends. Reading a long biography of Proust is certainly easier than reading *A la recherche du temps perdu.*

The relevance of the biographical approach to the literature of the last century is undeniable. Our experience is enriched by the knowledge that Victor Hugo's daughter was a poor swimmer and that Byron was fond of his sister. This is because much of the literature of romanticism and its immediate successors contains an important confessional component. The creative act is conceived as an act of self-expression; the author recreates his self, with important modifications, in his work, thereby writing pseudo-autobiography. 'Madame Bovary, c'est moi,' said Flaubert. We are invited to consider the work as an act of self-expression. The author has poured his heart out, what do we think of the results? 'Dans ce livre atroce j'ai mis tout mon coeur, toute ma haine, toute ma religion ...' wrote Baudelaire of *Les Fleurs du Mal.*

Ducasse wants his readers to relate to his works not as acts of self-expression, but as texts. *Les Chants de Maldoror* have nothing to do with confessional literature. Lest we suppose for a moment that they are the personalised expression of a belief in the beauties of evil, the joys of buggery, lest we believe that his sole purpose is to outdo Baudelaire, Ducasse wrote a second work.

The direct complement to *Les Chants de Maldoror*, it is entitled *Poésies Un* and *Poésies Deux*. It is the radical negation of everything that *Les Chants de Maldoror* stood for. It preaches total orthodoxy, total morality. It suggests that the greatest literary achievement of the Western world is the school speech-day prize. With this work, in every way as extreme as his first, the author makes it clear that his writing is not to be thought of

12

as a signed act of self-expression. The pseudonyms of *Les Chants de Maldoror* and the contradictory role of *Poésies* combine to inform us that Ducasse is absent from these works. He is covering a broader canvas than the self, utterly opposed to the concept of art as 'doing your own thing', a concept which he regards as a sign of the sentimental decrepitude of the post-romantic world.

He makes this clear in *Poésies* when he attacks the major figures of romanticism for their view of literature as self-expression. He draws up a list of the 'Grandes-Têtes-Molles' of his era, which includes Chateaubriand, Rousseau, Hugo, Poe, Maturin, George Sand, Goethe, Lermontov, Lamartine and Byron. He makes a more specific assault on the romantic aesthetic when he writes:

> Personal poetry has had its day ... Let us take up the indes-tructible thread of impersonal poetry, so violently snapped since the birth of the failed philosopher of Ferney, the abortion of the great Voltaire.[1]

He dates the origins of this conception of literature at the end of the seventeenth century. It might be more accurate to see its beginnings in Rousseau's *Confessions.* In the eighteenth century the writer was still a professional man of letters, a savant or a dilettante, writing less to express himself than to meet the demands of a public. He was not so much an artist as an artisan.

It is the romantic movement that first shapes the modern view of the artist as lone genius, starving in a garret and waiting for the inspiration that will provide him with a master-piece of his own. We have come to accept as a truth that knows no barriers of time or space, the fact that that there is a class of person known as artists, who, whether they work in Stone-Age caves, or on the French Riviera, are all the same kind of people doing the same kind of thing for the same kind of reason. Blessed with genius they are the victims of a daemonic vision which they must express, at all costs, for themselves alone.

Lautréamont provides us with the sober reminder that this conception of genius is just over a century old, and the product of romanticism. It was the romantics who first revealed an interest in 'personal art'. This can be seen in the new importance they attached to signature. Signature renders the work of art the expression of one man's vision; ceasing to be a thing in itself, it becomes the reflection of the personality of the man behind it. It is this shift from work to signature that accounts for the phenomenon of biographical criticism. The new importance of signature for the romantic generation is confirmed by a fascinating passage in the *Mémoires* of Berlioz. He recalls his sense of indignation when, as a young student at the Paris Conservatory, he discovered that conductors of the preceding generation would re-write passages of Mozart and Weber to suit either their own taste or the talents of their orchestra.[2] It is not the indignation of Berlioz that is interesting, but the fact that the earlier, classically-trained generation did not share his reverence for signature. They treated the composition as an object that they were free to use as they thought fit. It was only the romantic generation that was to treat the work of art as a sacred cow, believing that the artist's signature imposed an unbreakable seal.

The confessional bias of romantic art, its emphasis on qualities such as emotional authenticity, its shift from collective to personal values, and indeed its veritable invention of the concept of the individual, all originate with Rousseau. He is the first author to claim that he writes for himself alone. It is not for nothing that he describes the creative act in terms he also applies to his pet vice of masturbation. They are both a 'deadly substitute', surrogates for real-life experience.

Ducasse seeks a break with this tradition of literature as masturbation—doing your own thing. In *Poésies* he coined a phrase that was to become a surrealist slogan, marking the end of literature as an exquisite private experience: 'Poetry must be made by all, not by one.'[3]

The author's own indictment of confessional literature accounts for the lowly status to which the biography of Ducasse has here been relegated. If we are to do justice to the work we must approach it in terms that do justice to its impersonal nature. The sheer insignificance of the author's life provides an added inducement to regard his work as writing without a history. Indeed, it is to a certain extent even independent of its historical context. The original edition of *Poésies* never went on sale, and only became generally known on publication in the surrealist journal *Littérature* in 1923.

We know practically nothing about Ducasse except what he wrote. He left us a corpus of writing with a unique status. It seems designed to function impersonally: not as an act of self-expression, but rather as the unfolding of the basis of all conceivable acts of self-expression. Ducasse is not concerned to tell us what he thinks, but to create a text, an object designed to show us how we all think.

The only writing in any way comparable in its objectives is the poetry of Mallarmé. Mallarmé did not regard a poem as an act of self-expression, but rather as a contribution towards an attempt to echo the essential structure of the universe. What he described as *L'Oeuvre*, a term taken from alchemy, was to be something far outreaching the restrictions of individual consciousness—the *explication orphique de la terre*. Mallarmé, who was obsessed with etymological meaning, also thought of *explication* as an unfolding. He sought a means of expression that would create something universal: not just the description of individual objects and phenomena, but the basis of all conceivable objects and phenomena.

Lautréamont is seeking something very similar. However he wishes to describe not things in themselves, but the way in which we perceive them. He concentrates on the way the cultural grid filters our perceptions and shapes our sense of reality. His interest is very similar to that of Michel Foucault, a contemporary French philosopher. In his book *The Order of Things* he writes the history of what he terms the *épistème*, the basic element that orders our processes of cognition and categorisation. He shows the way that it has altered its nature over the course of four centuries. From his account we come to see how it is that the épistème determines the nature of what we can know, of what we accept and reject from the input of our sense data.

Lautréamont is interested in the épistème as a poet, not as a philosopher. He is not concerned with intellectual niceties. As a poet he simply tries to put across the sinister truth that we have been programmed—and that there is no programme without a programmer.

In order to convey this conviction he makes us step back from our society, its preconceptions and its stereotypes. He suggests a way of thinking about it that does not automatically endorse its values. Instead he establishes, objectively, just what those values are.

This is the kind of work done by anthropologists among primitive societies. It requires years of training to enable an outsider to compose a careful and accurate account of a foreign culture. Yet it is easier to describe other cultures than to describe your own. It takes a poet to do that. Lautréamont provides us with an aid to self-description. The challenge his work offers to our fundamental assumptions helps us to become our own anthropologists, and shows us that the field in which we work is quite as savage and ritualistic as any tribal culture.

CHAPTER TWO

The Life of Isidore Ducasse

The little we know about the life of Isidore Ducasse tells us practically nothing about the author of *Les Chants de Maldoror* and *Poésies*. What follows therefore is a brief life of Ducasse that has little to do with his poetry.

His father, François, was born in the Hautes-Pyrénées in 1809. He spent his early working life as a schoolmaster before emigrating to Uruguay, where he married Jacquette Davezac. It would seem that the marriage took place shortly before the birth of their eldest child Isidore, on 4 April 1846. The country was at that time in the throes of a bloody war with Argentina, in the course of which the capital sustained an eight-year siege at the hands of the Argentine dictator Manuel Rosas. During much of this time Ducasse, who had abandoned teaching to work in the French consulate, was in charge of the French legation.

Isidore was born in wartime. Although the war came to an end in 1852, his childhood was spent in a period of political unrest, interspersed with a number of epidemics. One source, probably unreliable, says that his mother took her own life a year and eight months after his birth.

We catch occasional glimpses of his father over the years. He features in chancery records where he is sometimes praised for his zeal. We know absolutely nothing about the first thirteen years in the life of his son, who returned to France in his fourteenth year, in 1859. From 1859 to 1862 Isidore was a boarder at the Lycée Impérial of Tarbes, a small town in south-west France. Diligent research has ascertained that in his first year he did well in Latin prose and grammar, got second prize in mathematics and a first prize for drawing. In his second year he was commended for general attitude, and got first prize for Latin prose, grammar and drawing. In his third year he was commended for general attitude, got first prizes for arithmetic, geometry and drawing, and was commended for Latin prose, unseen and grammar.

In 1863 he moved to a school in Pau, where he remained for two years. His master in the fifth form was a certain Gustave Hinstin, of whom more later, his classmates included Paul Lespès and Georges Minvielle. All three feature among the dedicatories of *Poésies*.

In his first year he was commended for classical recitation and got a second prize for English. In his second year he was commended for physics. He did not take the school-leavers' examination.

There are no records for his next three years. We then find him a writer, in Paris. The first printing of the first canto of *Les Chants* took place in August 1868. It reappears in a collection of poems submitted to a poetry contest in Bordeaux. The contest was in fact a phoney, a means of drumming up business for the printer.

The publication of the complete version of *Les Chants* was announced for 1869 by a broadsheet advertising clandestine books. But when it came to the point the Belgian printers, Lacroix and Verboeckhoven, doubtless mindful of the trouble that *Madame Bovary* and *Les Fleurs du Mal* had brought to perfectly innocent booksellers, decided against it, and it only went on sale in 1874. The edition had largely been financed by Ducasse himself. He complained of his bad luck to his bankers, in one of his few surviving letters. His father was apparently cutting off his funds, possibly as a result of his excessive interest in literature. He does not write warmly of his father:

> You have put into action the deplorable system of mistrust vaguely advocated by the eccentricities of my father; but you will have realised that my aching head does not prevent me from giving my attention to the difficult position in which you have been placed by a sheet of paper from South America, which has as its principal shortcoming a lack of clarity; for I do not take account of the offensive tone of certain melancholic remarks which one can easily forgive an old man, and which appeared, when I first read them,

18

intended henceforward to oblige you to exceed your duties as a banker towards a gentleman who has come to live in the capital.[1]

The only contemporary review of his work appears in an insignificant journal, *La Jeunesse*. Although it concerns the first canto alone, and misses much of the point, it is by no means unfavourable, regarding the piece as an extreme statement of romantic malaise: a one-sided view, but one shared by a number of later admirers. We have a few other letters to bankers and publishers, in one of which he claims to have:

... sung the praises of evil as did Mickiewicz, Byron, Milton, Southey, Musset, Baudelaire. Of course I exaggerated a bit, in order to make an original contribution to the kind of sublime literature that only sings of despair in order to depress the reader and make him long for goodness as a remedy.[2]

These lines, reading as they do as a parody of Baudelaire's apologetic defence of *Les Fleurs du Mal*, must have been written with the tongue lodged firmly in the cheek. The same letter contains an important phrase that points to the relationship between *Les Chants* and *Poésies*: '[In *Les Chants*] the moral is not yet complete.'[3] This is presumably because its viewpoint is yet to be complemented by *Poésies*, in every way an equal and an opposite force. The second book was published under the name of Isidore Ducasse, early in 1870. Again the work was undertaken at the author's expense.

Isidore Ducasse died at home on 4 November 1870, during the siege of Paris. We know no more about his death. We cannot even say whether we know so little at his own choice, or because of the confusion caused by the siege. His death was quite uneventful, nothing so dramatic as a suicide, a request for more light or even a protracted summer holiday in Abyssinia. His abandonment of literature is both total and totally anonymous, with no element of self-display.

Although Ducasse has practically no biography, he has biographers, and they are ingenious. A three-hundred page life has recently been published in France.[4] It scarcely adds a single fact to the little that is known about him, but rather is a biography such as Nabokov or Borges might have written. It is based entirely on what someone in Ducasse's situation might have experienced: the reconstruction of the life he may have had.

The only genuine documentary evidence we possess that tells us anything at all about Ducasse was compiled by his schoolfriend Paul Lespès. At the age of 81 he recalled what he could of Ducasse, the growing reputation of the author of *Les Chants* having finally overtaken him. Much of the value of his account derives from what it reveals of the straight reaction to Lautréamont. Indeed the status of these memoirs as a nonevent is admirably illustrated by a photograph in Marcelin Pleynet's excellent *Lautréamont par lui-même*. It shows a class of hirsute French schoolboys and its caption reads: 'A fifth-form group without Isidore Ducasse'. Nevertheless since this is the only portrait of any kind whatsoever that we possess, and since it contains at least one point of major interest, it is worth quoting in detail:

> I knew Ducasse at school ... I can see him now, a tall thin young man with a slight stoop. Pale with long hair falling across his forehead, and a shrill voice. There was nothing attractive about his person.
>
> He was usually sad, quiet and withdrawn. Once or twice he spoke to me in some excitement about countries overseas where life was free and happy.
>
> In class he would often spend whole hours with his elbows on the desk and his head in his hands, staring at a text-book without reading it. He was obviously day-dreaming ...
>
> In class he sometimes showed a keen interest in the teaching of Gustave Hinstin, a brilliant fifth-form master. He was very fond of Racine and Corneille, and particularly of Sophocles' *Oedipus Rex*. He found the scene in which Oedipus learns the terrible truth, utters cries of anguish and curses his destiny with his eyes torn out, very fine. He was only sorry that Jocasta did not crown the tragic horror by committing suicide on stage!
>
> He admired Edgar Poe ...
>
> At school we thought him prone to fantasy and daydreaming, but basically a good sort, no more than averagely bright, perhaps because he was behind in his work. One day

he showed me some poetry he had written. As far as I could judge the rhythm seemed a little odd and the ideas were obscure . . .

There seemed to be things that he refused to understand in case he lost some of his aversions and his scorn . . .

In the height of summer the pupils went swimming in the stream at Bois-Louis. It was a treat for Ducasse who was an excellent swimmer.

He told me one day that he really needed to cool his diseased brain in the spring water more often . . .

Towards the end of the school year Hinstin, who had already rebuked Ducasse for his so-called extravagances of thought and style, read out one of his essays.

The first sentences, which were very solemn, made him laugh, but soon he grew angry. Ducasse had not changed his style, he had exaggerated it. Never before had he given such free rein to his wild imagination. Each sentence was built up of strings of images, incomprehensible metaphors, and was rendered obscure by expressions and turns of style that were not always grammatically correct.

Hinstin, an orthodox classicist, whose penetrating critical sense never missed a single lapse of taste, took it to be a provocative act directed at the classical system, a bad joke at the teacher's expense. Unlike his usual indulgent self, he made Ducasse stay in after class. This punishment hurt him deeply; he complained bitterly to me and my friend Georges Minvielle. We did not even try to make him see that he'd gone much too far.

At school in the fifth and sixth forms Ducasse never showed any talent for mathematics and geometry, the fascinating beauties of which he celebrated so enthusiastically in *Les Chants*. But he did enjoy natural history. The animal kingdom excited his curiosity . . . Knowing that Minvielle and I were keen shots from childhood, he sometimes asked us about the habits and haunts of various Pyrenean birds, and about the way they flew.

Lespès goes on to tell how he received an anonymous complimentary copy of the first edition of *Les Chants* and immediately assumed that Ducasse had written it. He continues:

At school he saw more of Georges Minvielle and myself than of the others. But his aloofness, his scornful solemnity and a certain stand-offishness, the obscure questions that he would urgently ask us, and which we were quite unable to answer, his ideas, his style, the extravagance which our excellent teacher Hinstin was in the habit of pointing out, above all his groundless fits of bad temper, in short all his strangeness, made us feel that he was somewhat unbalanced.

La folle du logis appeared once and for all in a French speech in which he piled up a frightening plethora of the most horrible images of death. It was nothing but broken bones, hanging guts, bleeding or pulped flesh. It was the recollection of this speech that made me recognise the author of *Les Chants de Maldoror* some years later, even though Ducasse had never talked of his literary plans.

Ducasse was very hurt by Hinstin's reproaches. He was convinced that he had written an excellent speech full of original ideas and fine expressions. Of course if you compare *Les Chants de Maldoror* with *Poésies* you might think that Ducasse was not sincere. But if, as I believe, he was sincere at school, why might he not have been so later, when he tried to become a poet in prose, and his deluded imagination persuaded him that the image of a delight in evil might lure lost souls despairing of hope and virtue back to the fold.

At school we thought him a good sort, but a bit, how shall I say, cracked. He was not immoral; there was nothing sadistic about him.[5]

This portrait shows us a number of stock responses to the writing. For example it dismisses allegations of insincerity. *Of course* Ducasse was sincere and well-meaning, despite his countless protestations to the contrary. It was just that he had these headaches and was, well, a bit potty. The work is absolved from meaning what it says, in order to establish that there was nothing actually bad about Ducasse; he was no sadist, just somewhat eccentric. It is of the utmost significance that Lespès should have used the term *la folle du logis* (roughly, 'the resident madwoman') to describe the imagination. This characteristic term of denigration was the product of the classical spirit, which saw the imagination as a source of agreeable ornament, which might enliven passages of reality-oriented prose, but which, if abused, would lead you straight to bedlam. The classical doctrine of *rien de trop* applies above all to the imagination. *La folle* must know her place. Of course Ducasse was not serious—it was just his imagination.

Another important aspect of the dismissive turn is Lespès' almost exclusive attention to Ducasse's use of language. He talks of his exotic word-patterns, his lack of stylistic restraint, his plethora of images. Because Ducasse is an old friend, Lespès is anxious to safeguard his memory, and loyally dismisses *Les Chants* as a verbal extravaganza; six cantos of wild oats which may make a lot of noise, but which do not matter, as they do not mean anything. Moreover we need not take the homosexual eroticism too seriously, because, as Lespès so delicately points out, there was nothing queer about old Isidore.

Lespès employs the argument *ad hominem* to exonerate what the man has written from meaning what it says. Ducasse's memory remains intact, and his work remains a curiosity. Had he lived he would no doubt have put childish things behind him and settled down. In the meantime it would be unfair to take his adolescent indiscretions seriously.

To do him justice, it must be admitted that Lespès provides one invaluable insight into the way that Ducasse may have developed his understanding of the oppressive nature of his culture. Cultural oppression begins in the schoolroom. This point is made by the sociologist Jules Henry, whose *Culture Against Man* provides a hair-raising account of how the Great Society turns its junior citizens into consumers by the inculcation of its 'pecuniary ethic' from kindergarten on. It is in the schoolroom that individuals are first forced into the culture-pattern's adamantine mould:

> American classrooms, like educational institutions anywhere, express the values, preoccupations, and fears found in the culture as a whole. School has no choice; it must train the children to fit the culture as it is. School can give training in skills; it cannot teach creativity.[6]

Hinstin taught Ducasse the formalised stylistics of official French, and kept him in after hours when he tried to write poetry:

23

The function of education has never been to free the mind and the spirit of man, but to bind them; and to the end that the mind and spirit of his children should never escape *Homo sapiens* has employed praise, ridicule, admonition, accusation, mutilation and even torture to chain them to the culture-pattern ... Were young people truly creative the culture would fall apart, for originality, by definition, is different from what is given, and what is given is the culture itself. From the endless, pathetic, 'creative hours' of kindergarten to the most abstruse problems in sociology and anthropology, the function of education is to prevent the truly creative intellect from getting out of hand.[7]

Small wonder that Lespès and his friends found Ducasse no more than averagely bright and a bit odd into the bargain. Ducasse commits the schoolboy's deadly sin. He refuses to buy the system; he declines the tasteful stylistic models of Hinstin. The conclusion is obvious—he must be stupid:

... the child with a socially creative imagination will not be encouraged to play among new social systems, values, and relationships ... Furthermore, such a child will simply be unable to fathom the absurdities that seem transparent *truth* to the teacher. What idiot believes in the 'law of supply and demand', for example? But the children who do tend to *become* idiots, and learning to be an idiot is part of growing up! Or, as Camus puts it, learning to be *absurd*. Thus the child who finds it impossible to learn to think the absurd the truth, who finds it difficult to accept absurdity as a way of life, the intellectually creative child whose mind makes him flounder like a poor fish in the net of absurdities flung around him in school, usually comes to think himself stupid.[8]

Hinstin looks on Ducasse's written work as senseless, but, more important, it is also an attempt to rock the boat. Such boys are dangerous. In order to bring the lad to heel he employs the schoolmaster's two most effective weapons. He keeps him in— the culture-pattern restricts the liberty of those who fail to conform. He exposes him to ridicule—better to write like a lawyer's clerk than feel a fool. Henry describes how the system encourages children to practise 'carping criticism' of each other's work, to maximise their sense of conformity and their competitive drive:

> It stands to reason that a competitive system must do this; and adults, since they are always tearing each other to pieces, should understand that children will be no different. School is indeed a training for later life not because it teaches the three Rs (more or less), but because it instils the essential cultural nightmare fear of failure, envy of success, and absurdity.[9]

Ducasse can be seen to encounter the oppressive force of culture in the classroom. He is forced to become something he is not. The traumatic nature of this experience has been used to instigate yet another of the great dismissive critiques of Lautréamont. Gaston Bachelard, usually one of the most inspiring of all critics of French poetry, appears to try to explain away Lautréamont's work as the ravings of a vindictive schoolboy suffering from a *complexe de rhétorique*, fifth-form histrionics. The criticism is all the more damaging for being a half-truth. Ducasse learnt about cultural oppression in school as we can tell from the following:

> When a boarder, in a lycée, is ruled for years, that are centuries, from morning to night and from night to morning, by a pariah of civilisation, who always has his eye on him, he feels a living hatred billowing like thick vapours up into his mind which seems about to burst. From the moment he was cast into prison, to the coming moment when he will be free, a raging fever makes his face yellow, knits his brows and makes rings beneath his eyes.[10]

But Bachelard's criticism is misleading since it confuses cause and effect. Ducasse experienced education as imprisonment, it is true. But to say this is not to reveal the full meaning of *Les Chants*. It simply tells us of the circumstances in which Ducasse first encountered cultural repression. Bachelard was himself perhaps too much part of the French educational system to be able to accept what Lautréamont, as opposed to Ducasse, might have to say. Lacking the necessary detachment he had to reject the work.

The only other work written in the nineteenth century that

can match *Les Chants* on its principal counts of an absurd, cruel and precise logic, set in a world of black humour and automatic violence, was also born in the schoolroom, in protest against the pedagogic authority of a schoolmaster-God. Alfred Jarry's *Ubu Roi*, one of the funniest plays in the French language, was originally intended as a satire against a singularly oppressive master. It developed into the dominant strain of Jarry's work: a black and absurd protest against the world at large.

Neither Jarry nor Ducasse possessed the conceptual clarity of a sociologist, but both realised, as poets, that it is in the schoolroom that we are compelled to accept the conventions of our culture-pattern as if these were immutable natural laws. It is there that culture blinds us with the big lie which tells us that the world is made as the culture chooses to regard it.

CHAPTER THREE

Le Comte de Lautréamont and the Media I

Some ingenious theories have been advanced to explain Ducasse's *nom de plume*. It has been suggested that the name means 'L'autre est Amon'—the Egyptian God of Light. Alternatively, 'L'autre est à mont'—on a mountain or on high. At all events the first syllable certainly points to the most important theme in the book; the interplay between *Le Même* and *L'Autre*, like and unlike. It is through these categories of similarity and difference that the grid operates, and to understand how we handle them is to understand the way in which we form our vision of reality.

The association of otherness with a divine figure is found throughout *Les Chants*. Maldoror the homosexual, who must have 'beings that resemble me', mounts a savage attack on God who is described as the very embodiment of otherness—'le grand objet extérieur'. In the final analysis virtually every word that Ducasse ever wrote is designed to articulate the range and limitations of a world-view conceived in terms of like and unlike.

The name Lautréamont contains yet another layer of meaning, one which points to the important part played in this work by parody and plagiarism. The author has an extremely sophisticated approach to borrowing. Just as he rejects the notion of literature as self-expression, so he rejects the equally romantic notion of the work of art as something unique and utterly original. Of course, in an absolute sense, there can be no such thing as an utterly original work of art. In one way or another the artist always builds on the artistic conventions he inherits. But on the whole artists tend to assimilate and rework their sources in such a way that these are no longer apparent on the surface of their work.

In this respect, as in so many others, Ducasse goes to the opposite extreme. Far from concealing his sources, he makes them as conspicuous as he can. Large sections of *Poésies* consist

27

of passages lifted wholesale from Pascal and Vauvenargues: a word is changed here, a negative omitted there, and the borrowings come to mean something quite different. In these word-games we see the author's obsessive interest in the interaction of form and sense. It is *Poésies* that contain the crucial slogan that champions plagiarism:

> Plagiarism is necessary. Progress implies it. It follows an author's sentence closely, uses his expressions, deletes a false idea and replaces it with a correct one.[1]

Lautréamont places his work quite openly under the sign of plagiarism. Among his more or less consciously avowed sources we find: the Bible, Baudelaire, Byron, Dante, Flaubert, Goethe, Homer, Hugo, Maturin, Musset, Poe, Scott, Eugène Süe, and Wagner. This technique of barefaced parody has the effect of placing *Les Chants* and *Poésies* in a certain relationship to tradition. They stand to one side of the mainstream of European literature; not part of it, but referring to it. By means of his parodies Ducasse redefines our view of the works he echoes, reshaping our view of our cultural heritage and transforming the past. *Les Chants* become the source of our view of Byron or Baudelaire, as opposed to their being the source of *Les Chants*.

With the name Lautréamont Ducasse brings out a crucial affiliation between *Les Chants* and nineteenth-century fiction. Whatever the other implications of his *nom de plume*, we may be sure of one thing; Le Comte de Lautréamont is a character who has stepped out of the pages of the popular novel. Neither real nor imaginary, he is born of literature, for his ancestor was a character created by the novelist Eugène Süe.

Süe was the first writer of popular bestsellers in the modern sense. He was closely associated with a major breakthrough in the marketing and merchandising of fiction, since he was one of the first French authors to have his work published in serial form in the new popular press. His novels accordingly acquired a tremendous impact on the popular imagination, roughly comparable to the first radio and TV soap-operas. He rightly became known as *Le Roi du Roman Populaire*. He was the first European novelist to become so well known that his name was a household word synonymous with the novel itself. With

Süe the novel became a mass medium and a broadly based cultural force.

In 1837 Süe published a historical novel, *Lautréamont*. Its hero, Jules Duhamel de Latréamont, apparently based on a historical character, was a brutal, insolent officer, with a black and cynical sense of humour and distinctly mephistophelian characteristics. He plotted assiduously against the French monarchy, the representative of law and order, both during and after the Fronde. The assault on established authority and the character of Süe's hero both have affinities with the feeling tone of *Les Chants*.

It is quite understandable that Ducasse should draw our attention to the popular novel. Anyone seeking, towards the end of the last century, to make a statement about the culture of his age was obliged to think about the medium of the novel. The classic example is Flaubert. His two major novels of contemporary life deal with the impact of reality upon characters who derived their impressions of reality from novels. Emma Bovary has formed her world-view by reading second-rate novelettes. She moves through life in a media-induced dream, eternally discontent because she fails to experience the satisfactions which her reading has persuaded her are hers by right. Her reaction is: 'This cannot be real because it is not like the book; reality must lie somewhere else.' Frédéric Moreau, the hero of *L'Education sentimentale*, suffers from a similar delusion, although his sufferings are less crudely motivated. As a rich young provincial who comes to live in the capital, he feels the world should be at his feet, that he should re-enact the meteoric rise of one of Balzac's young heroes. But he finds that Paris has none of the super-charged vitality of Balzac's world. Flaubert writes about people who believe what they read in books, who confuse the medium with the real thing.

The increasing importance of the novel in the nineteenth century is an echo of the transformation of European society from a feudal aristocracy to a bourgeois, mercantile meritocracy. Where tragedy, in the seventeenth century, dealt with eternal absolute values of heroism—the aesthetic of a warrior class that modelled itself on supermen—the novel lowers its sights, shows men not as they might be but as they are, defines them not by their passionate extremes but by their workaday reality. It places them in their everyday context, situates them squarely in their physical environment, and defines them in terms of where they are as much as, if not more than, in terms of who they are.

Above all the novel holds up a looking-glass to the literate middle classes. It forms their sense of identity, defines them in terms of their role and situation. As an art form it represents a departure from the aesthetic of classicism. The classical experience had two essential components. In the first place it was a transcendent aesthetic. The protagonists of classicism rose above themselves and their emotions, they exceeded their destinies and overrode the limitations of their humanity. Secondly, the classical experience was a group experience. Its public took its pleasures collectively in the public space of the theatre. This was consistent with a culture-pattern which had no room for privacy, in which courtiers could be seen urinating against the palace walls and the Sun King would receive ambassadors on a commode. In high classicism even the novel formed part of this public experience. The most important novel of the seventeenth century, *La Princesse de Clèves*, was a work that was enjoyed collectively : the heroine's dilemma—should she or should she not tell her husband that she was in love with another man—was the enduring topic for discussion in the *salons*. Even the novel, a form essentially foreign to the classical aesthetic, was treated in classical terms.

The novel makes a break with classicism because it echoes the need for privacy, and because it is essentially anti-transcendental, anti-cathartic. Its perspectives furnish a valet's eye view of heroism—consider Tolstoy's treatment of Napoleon in *War and Peace*. The novel works too much in close-up, handles too much detail, for it to have the nobility of tragedy. The anti-cathartic nature of the novel, that titillates our emotions rather than purging them, is confirmed by the fact that the novel is the great pornographic medium, and the eighteenth century, which saw the rise of the novel, was pornography's golden age. It is the business of pornography to maintain the reader in a perpetually aroused condition. In such a situation going too far is quite as counter-productive as not going far enough. The suitability of the novel as a pornographic medium confirms its essentially anti-transcendental bent. It is the ideal form for writing cliff-hangers—hence the novels of Richardson, some of the greatest sexual cliff-hangers of all time. Its pornographic role also points to another of its characteristics: that it is for private consumption.

Privacy is essentially a middle-class project. It has nothing to do with an aristocracy that, like Voltaire's Mme du Châtelet, does not mind undressing in front of its valets. Only with the rise of the middle class do we find a great emphasis on domestic and private values. The public spaces of eighteenth-century salons, designed for debate and conversation, become transformed into the nooks and crannies of a Victorian drawing-room, designed to permit the co-existence of a series of separate activities.

The novel meets this new-found demand for privacy. It leaves the reader isolated, alone with his dream-machine. He can turn it on or off at will, make it run at the speed he wants. It needs no power, no dependence on others to set it in motion. The image of the reader of novels, alone and engrossed, is the very emblem of the aesthetic consumer of the romantic and post-romantic era.

The novel reigns supreme throughout the period beginning with Rousseau's *Julie,* the first novel to impress itself on the European consciousness, and ending with Proust's *A la recherche du temps perdu,* when the novel becomes too difficult to remain a popular form. Within this period virtually every important piece of creative writing takes the form of a novel. The two poetic masterpieces of the century, Pushkin's *Eugene Onegin* and Baudelaire's *Les Fleurs du Mal,* may both be thought of as novels. Pushkin's piece is manifestly a novel in verse, whereas Baudelaire's work is a carefully arranged mosaic tracing an unmistakable narrative pattern. The novel can, moreover, be seen to treat themes and preoccupations previously the reserve of tragedy. Stendhal's *Le Rouge et le Noir* could quite properly be described as the tragedy of Julien Sorel; he is an outsider, and the novel portrays the conflict between society and the private self, which finds its Hamletic resolution in Sorel's acquiescence to a sentence of death that is tantamount to suicide. The novels of Dostoevsky are even closer to tragedy. He is in many ways comparable to Lautréamont, since he deals with the transgression of taboos that are the very constituents of society. 'We all desire our father's death,' says Ivan

Karamazov. None more than the trinity of Ducasse, Lautréamont and Maldoror.

The prominence of the code of the novel in nineteenth-century culture may explain its role in *Les Chants*. The work consists of episodes that might have been taken from various novels—stories or sketches of a central character, Maldoror, and his fight against God. It may well be the author's interest in narrative fiction that explains his choice of prose as opposed to verse.

An examination of the construction of *Les Chants* confirms the important role of the novel-form. The work consists of six cantos. The first five are made up of more or less fantastic episodes, interspersed with lyrical digressions. Although they all feature Maldoror, they lack continuity. They contain a series of images and situations which, as we shall see, are brought to a definitive conclusion in the final canto, drawing the entire work together. The author describes this as the 'analytic part of the work', consisting of a 'little thirty-page novel'.

The last canto recounts a coherently developed situation, making use of devices commonly associated with the Gothick novel. Unlike the earlier cantos it both uses and parodies the novel's narrative code. It is through this code that the author finds the definitive version of images and situations that have remained embryonic in the first five cantos. He says so in so many words:

> I believe that after a few false starts I have finally found my definitive formula. It is the best since it is the novel.[2]

In the light of hindsight it would seem that no other formula could have served. The novel was *the* characteristic form of the period and its use immediately brings into play the entire nineteenth-century literary tradition.

Why should the author select a name that alludes to the popular novel, more particularly to what is known as the *roman noir*, a term that includes both the Gothick or supernatural form and the penny-dreadful ancestor of the modern thriller? Süe was the great author of *romans noirs*. Some of his works such as *The Wandering Jew* contained a strong supernatural element, whereas his masterpiece *Les Mystères de Paris* was much closer to the thriller form. Indeed the modern thriller is the direct inheritor of the Gothick tradition. It uses all the Gothick stock-in-trade: mysterious atmosphere, inexplicable conjunctures of circumstance, unsolved riddles and enigmas, tremendous complications of plot and an emphasis on melodrama at all costs. But in contrast with works of hard-line Gothick such as *The Monk, Melmoth the Wanderer* or *The Saragossa Manuscript*, which rely for their resolutions and effects upon the supernatural, and which have their descendants in the fantasies of writers such as Lord Dunsany, H. P. Lovecraft and Mervyn Peake, the tensions and mysteries of the secular thriller are resolved by a detective, admittedly of quasi-superhuman powers, who eventually provides a rational explanation to account for events that have hitherto appeared to defy all reason.

In the absence of other evidence, the only clue to why Lautréamont should have used this form is provided by comparable attitudes in other authors. Dostoevsky, for example, adopted a code founded on Gothick horror, suspense and the detective story. His four major novels, *Crime and Punishment, The Idiot, The Possessed* and *The Brothers Karamazov,* all have murder as their centrepiece. *Crime and Punishment* represents one of the classic variants of the detective story, showing us events through the eyes of the killer. *The Idiot* comes to a climax with Rogozhin's murder of Nastasya Filipovna, and the collapse into imbecility of his *alter ego,* Prince Myshkin. *The Possessed* features a para-political assassination, an enforced suicide and a lynching. The central theme of *The Brothers Karamazov* is parricide. The novel contains a crucial trial scene, showing how a technically innocent man is convicted on the basis of an overwhelming body of circumstantial evidence.

Dostoevsky uses the plot structure of the suspense novel. He used to publish in serial form, and his work reflects the demands of its medium. He deliberately withholds crucial information in order to build tension—driving home the point by telling us as much. We always feel that his narrative only illuminates a portion of the picture: part, perhaps the most important part, is bathed in shadow. The world of Dostoevsky has none of the patrician serenity of Tolstoy, none of his rounded, complete characters, portrayed so vividly that they come alive. Dostoevsky describes a world of absolute need, inhabited by

33

stylised grotesques, with violent and yet ritualistic reactions and expressions; their features distorted by twisted smiles that are choked off by a madman's cry or an epileptic fit. He plays on the sentimental emotions and takes delight in the depiction of extraordinary suffering and poverty. Daughters become whores 'in order to support their starving families and tubercular mothers. Such pathetic passages are usually attested as evidence of Dostoevsky's humanitarian compassion. But so drastic are his appeals to our sense of pity that, particularly when looked at through the grid of Lautréamont, he sometimes seems to be plucking at our heart-strings with a sadist's touch.

Dostoevsky chose to write in this manner because he found it convenient to use existing literary forms. By echoing the language of contemporary fiction he made his work accessible to anyone with contemporary tastes. His novels spoke in the language of their times, even though they used it to say something quite new. Lautréamont seems to adopt Gothick forms for similar reasons. He uses the formulae of melodrama to depict Maldoror, and this renders the central character accessible to anyone familiar with the enormously popular *littérature noire* from Mrs Radcliffe to Edgar Allan Poe.

This is not the effect of code alone however. Reference to Dostoevsky again brings out certain undercurrents. He is at pains to stress the fact that the events he describes, however extraordinary they might seem, are truly emblematic of his society. In *Crime and Punishment* the investigator describes Raskolnikov's murder as a crime of our times. It is as if the author deliberately adopts a language of melodrama, criminality and violence as the language that represents the world of soulless urbanised nineteenth-century Russia. In that respect Dostoevsky's code really does become his message, telling us that the choice of code is dictated by the taste of the age. The very popularity of that language of violence derived from the prominent part that violent death and sexual perversity played in the dream-life of his society.

Ducasse, born during a war, brought up in a capital in a state of siege, and dying during another, may well have drawn our attention to the popular novel because of its representative characteristics. Circumstantial evidence suggests that he was attuned to a climate of violence. He was, moreover, highly aware of the status of styles of writing as codes, ways of handling and rendering reality. In *Poésies* he attacks the romantics for the irreparable moral damage they inflicted upon their culture. He would seem to have realised that you can tell the nature of a culture from its art. The popular melodramatic novel was utterly representative of the society in which it was produced and consumed.

This suggests that Ducasse employs the language of the popular novel ironically. He would seem to suggest that because he writes fantasy—tales of rape, sadism, homosexual murder, of apocalyptic events such as God's visit to a brothel—the reader may be tempted to allow himself the luxury of a purely aesthetic thrill, reassuring himself with the thought that 'of course it isn't true'. But in a sense it is. Because the reader reads on, instead of throwing the book down in disgust, he makes those fantasies part of his dream, his cultural world. Moreover, since the incidents of *Les Chants* are all intensified versions of the most sought-after cultural pabulum of the period, Lautréamont drives home the point that what the *hypocrite lecteur* dismisses as mere fantasy is really a psychic pen-portrait of that reader's secret life.

CHAPTER FOUR

Le Comte de Lautréamont and the Media II

We derive our sense of reality not from first-hand experience, but very largely through the agency of the media. Consequently our sense of reality is shaped by what the media tell us:

> Very little of what we think we know of the social realities of the world have we found out first-hand. Most of the 'pictures in our heads' we have gained from these media—even to the point where we often do not really believe what we see before us until we read about it in the paper or hear about it on the radio. The media not only give us information; they guide our very experience. Our standards of credulity, our standards of reality, tend to be set by these media rather than by our own fragmentary experience.[1]

This not only applies to the news media, but to the arts. The arts do not create a seemingly direct account of reality, but something less tangible and a great deal more influential. They project the collective myth of their culture. They show us the world as we would like it to be, uncluttered by the contingencies and distortions of workaday reality. Their portrayals are mythic in that the arts represent a world of pure values that is larger than life, because it is simpler, cleaner, less adulterated by chance than real life can ever be. The reader who dismisses *Les Chants* as mere literature makes a colossal mistake. Literature is the stuff that life is made of, for a culture lives by and through its myths. Through those myths it views and interprets the world, and those who shape its myths bear a terrible burden. John Wayne's personal responsibility for the war in South-East Asia does not begin with *The Green Berets*. It starts some thirty years earlier with *Stagecoach*.

Ducasse makes it clear that his form is to be taken seriously when he writes:

> Appropriating a style that some will deem naive although it is

so profound, I will make it serve to interpret ideas which, alas, may not appear grandiose.[2]

He warns us not to dismiss his form as trivial. It is in fact profound, because it is to profoundly representative. For it is the popular art-forms, rather than the works of high seriousness, that capture the mythologies and value patterns of their age.

Accordingly, Ducasse makes great use of the naive style of popular fiction. The heroes of the Gothick novel were satanic figures described in the language of hysteria. We find them on horseback, swathed in black, riding at the gallop through storm-tossed nights. The early pages of *Les Chants* describe Maldoror in similar terms. Pale, dark and isolated, his face bears the scar of divine retribution: it was once struck by a thunder-bolt. Anyone familiar with hard-edge romanticism will recognise the tone of the following passage. It places Maldoror in the paradigm of Melmoth, Dracula and the Wandering Jew:

> He goes from country to country and everywhere he is shunned. Some say that he is the childhood victim of some hereditary madness. Others believe his extreme, instinctive cruelty shames even him, and caused his parents to die of grief. There are those who maintain that in his youth he was branded with a surname; that it has left him inconsolable for the rest of his life, for his injured pride saw in it the flagrant proof of man's malice, born with childhood and increasing over the years. That surname was *The Vampire*![3]

But by the time we reach the final canto the tone has changed. There is another atmosphere more typical of the *roman noir* in its later stages.

One of the most popular versions of the romantic hero-figure in its subsequent development is the Napoleon of crime. He is of course a direct descendant of the Faustian hero of early Gothick, but he has lost his direct affiliations with the supernatural. Balzac's Vautrin, as he appears in *Splendeurs et Misères des Courtisanes* is a case in point. He is virtually superhuman, no one can outwit him or match his strength. A master of intrigue, a genius at disguise, he foils the police at every turn. Vautrin represents a crucial turning point as the genre moves from the satanic villain condemned to an eternity of damnation, to the private eye, Chandler's knight in a grubby trench-coat, who is outside the law, because the law itself is corrupt. Vautrin first appears as a criminal making war on society only to appear, in his final incarnation, as chief of police.

This type of character filled European popular fiction of the next hundred years. A famous example was Fantômas; an arch-criminal of the *belle époque*, he was the subject of a great cult in the *avant-garde* before the First World War. His official fan-club counted Apollinaire and Picasso among its founder members. Edgar Wallace's *Four Just Men* represents a multiplication of the figure. There was also the popular double image of positive and negative heroes with equal intelligence and ingenuity which they employ to opposing ends: these are the famous Holmes and Moriarty, Bulldog Drummond and Carl Petersen, James Bond and Blofeld.

In the final canto Ducasse describes his hero in precisely this idiom:

> Maldoror well knew that the police, that bastion of civilisation, had been looking for him obstinately for years, and that a veritable army of spies and agents was constantly on his heels. Without, however, being able to find him. Such was his overwhelming skill that, as casually as you please, he could avoid traps which could not fail to succeed, thwart plans that bore witness to the most intelligent preparation. He had a particular talent for adopting appearances that rendered him unrecognisable to the most practised eye. Superior disguises, an artist would say. In this respect he verged on genius. Did you notice that graceful pretty cricket moving so briskly through the sewers of Paris? Maldoror! . . . Today he is in Madrid: tomorrow he will be in St Petersburg, yesterday he was in Pekin . . . Perhaps the bandit is seven hundred leagues away; perhaps he stands beside you.[4]

The language is quite different from that of the first portrait. The one quality they share is parody and exaggeration. Ducasse has made fascinating use of the novel form, embracing its principal aspects, Gothick and criminal, and arranging these in chronological order. He moves from the vampire to the Napoleon of crime, as the genre moves from Melmoth to

Fantômas. He parodies the full range of the genre and writes an account of its evolution into his parody.

He also makes use of the popular novel's narrative devices, notably the fundamental device of the enigma. The serial form of the popular novel encourages the extensive use of the enigma to end episodes. In its most extreme form it becomes the very basis of the detective story of the Agatha Christie or John Dickson Carr type. Here the murder creates a combination of circumstances which Hercule Poirot or Doctor Fell will resolve in the last chapter.

The device also serves as an episodic element within the body of the plot. In Conan Doyle's *The Speckled Band* a man is murdered in a locked room. As he dies he mutters something about a speckled band. It is of course Holmes who resolves the enigma. He discounts the possibility that the dying man was referring to a band of freckled gypsies, and eventually concludes that he must have been alluding to a speckled snake that had been introduced into the room. Much of the tension depends on the ambiguity of the word band, and our wondering what on earth the speckled band could be.

The surrealistic plot of Lautréamont's mini-novel makes abundant use of this device. Echoing the world of Süe, in whose works evil usually triumphs cynically over good, it describes Maldoror's sadistic murder of Mervyn, a well-mannered Anglo-Saxon adolescent, despite all God's efforts to thwart him.

The novel is divided into chapters, each one of which concludes with a cryptic sentence that reads as an arbitrary and absurd invention, but which subsequently proves to have a rational explanation. The author seems to be asking whether something ceases to be absurd simply because it can be explained. What does such explanation actually explain? Perhaps we delude ourselves when we are satisfied by a 'rational' account. The fact that two plus two equals four may prove that God's in his heaven, but, says Lautréamont, perhaps we should take a closer look at God.

These cryptic sentences have rational explanations that are no less surrealistic than the enigmas they resolve. Rationality has its own madness.

The first use of this device is very close to Dostoevsky's practice of telling us that explanations will come later. The author concludes a theoretical digression on the novel with the following:

> How could the Pont du Carrousel maintain its neutrality when it heard the piercing cries that seemed to come from the sack?[5]

In French the use of the definite article suggests that the nouns so qualified have already been introduced. The sense of pseudo-familiarity that results is an essential ingredient of the formula. The reader is made to feel that he has missed something, that he should be familiar with the circumstances in question, and this has the curious effect of increasing his involvement with what he reads. In Lautréamont's case an explanation comes later. Maldoror will arrange to meet Mervyn on the bridge. He does so, bundles him into a sack, swings it several times against the parapet and hands it to a butcher on his way to the abattoir, saying that it contains a more than usually heavy dog which he would like put down.

The next version of the device, which is a little stronger, is again introduced unexpectedly:

> Direct yourselves to the swan lake; I shall tell you in due course why one of the flock is completely black, and why its body, supporting an anvil that bears the rotting corpse of a crab, quite understandably inspires distrust in its aquatic comrades.[6]

This is explained, if that is the word, by subsequent events. The crab is an archangel sent by God in an attempt to thwart Maldoror. The villain outwits it, kills it with a stick, smashes it on an anvil which he ties to his back, and turns himself into a swan to hide in the middle of a flock. But Providence will not let him get away with it completely; it singles him out, ensuring that no swan will associate with him, by turning him black.

The final version of the device is more intricate and more extreme. Making a final nonsense of all explanation it reads:

> The fish-tail will, it is true, only fly for three days; but alas, the beam will still be burnt and a cylindro-conical bullet will pierce the skin of the rhinoceros, despite the snow-maiden and the beggar. For the crowned madman will have told the truth about the fidelity of the fourteen daggers.[7]

The fish-tail is the form taken by the archangel who is not dead after all. It flies for three days in search of help before Maldoror shoots it down with a poisoned arrow. Thereupon an old beam, its load-bearing days at an end, stands up in protest to the Lord, only to be informed that the archangel deserved to die. Maldoror burns the beam in punishment. The rhinoceros is in fact God attempting a last-minute rescue. But Maldoror, who is perched on top of the Colonne Vendôme, shoots Him, as He appears, panting, round the corner of the Rue Castiglione. The snow-maiden was the nickname of Mervyn's mother, who was equally helpless. The crowned madman turns out to be Maldoror's henchman, crowned with a chamber-pot. The four-teen daggers are stranger still. When discussing the final arrangements with the madman Maldoror inquires about the fourteen daggers, and is assured that they are faithful as ever.

Comedy apart, these parodies have a genuine function. Merciless exaggeration beyond the point of ridicule makes us see more 'realistic' versions of the device in a new light. Lautréamont compels us to look at them suspiciously. He emphasises that they are the mere products of a narrative code : a set of rules and habits that seem real simply because we are accustomed to accept them without question.

Such distortions make us realise that realism is relative; the product of a convention. The paintings of Giotto, which appear to us tremendously stylised, seemed so real to his contemporaries that they felt they could touch his angels. Similarly, much of what we take to be an accurate rendering of the world as reflected in fiction, is the result of our unquestioning acceptance of a convention, a code.

Ducasse implies that the kind of 'realistic novel' that begins 'La marquise sortit à cinq heures' is no less surrealistic and absurd, certainly no more real, than the fourteen daggers. It is just that we have grown accustomed to the convention. Such novels have come to form part of our culture-patterns, and we accept anything that fits those patterns as real. We forget that it is culture that has created our sense of reality.

Marshall McLuhan cites a fascinating illustration of this point : an article describing a primitive people's first encounter with a new language, the language of film. Some Africans were shown a documentary made specially for them, about how to keep down mosquitoes:

> ... in very slow time, very slow technique, of what would be required of an ordinary householder in a primitive African village, in getting rid of standing water—draining pools, picking up all empty tins ... and so forth. We showed this film to an audience and asked them what they had seen, and they said they had seen a chicken, a fowl, and we didn't know there was a fowl in it! So we very carefully scanned the frames one by one for this fowl, and sure enough, for about a second, a fowl went over the corner of the frame. Someone had frightened the fowl and it had taken flight, through the right-hand bottom segment of the frame. This was all that had been seen. The other things we had hoped they would pick up from the film they had not picked up at all, and they had picked up something which we didn't know was in the film until we inspected it minutely.[8]

The author describes the contents of the film. It lasted five minutes and had sequences such as that of a labourer emptying a tin that had water in it and placing it on a rubbish dump. The chicken appeared for a second in this kind of setting. All the audience said they saw on initial response was the chicken. They eventually admitted to having seen a man, but made no attempt to make a story out of it. Instead they inspected the frame for details. The author concludes:

> We found that the film is, as produced in the West, a very highly conventionalised piece of symbolism, *although it looks very real...*
>
> Panning shots were very confusing because the audience didn't realise what was happening. They thought that the items and details inside the picture were literally moving. The convention was not accepted.

Because the code of the film was utterly foreign to them they were quite unable to handle it. They were cinematic illiterates who saw the film as an incoherent jumble of images. But what is really revealing is that the author of the piece needed first-hand experience of this kind of communication-breakdown to understand that film, which he had always accepted as a more or less direct rendering of reality, was in fact a highly conventionalised language. It took an outsider's response to make him see it for what it was.

Laurtéamont makes us our own outsiders. He distorts and exaggerates the language of narrative to the point of absurdity and beyond, to show us that what we accept as real is in fact the product of a set of literary rules, their devices quite as arbitrary as any of his, and perhaps quite s absurd.

CHAPTER FIVE

Maldoror

Lautréamont describes his hero in the language of definitive defiance, as God's enemy. Along with the trappings of black romanticism he inherits its concomitant qualities of an impassive dandyism.

The dandy is one of the most important creations of nineteenth-century culture. His basic attitude is one of refusal. In a world in which everyone is grubbing for money, success or security, the dandy declines to dirty his hands. The metaphor of clean hands is brought to life by Eugène Süe. One of the definitive dandies of his time, he was never to be seen without a pair of spotless pale-pink gloves. He changed them several times a day and never wore the same pair twice. The dandy expresses scorn for the values of the pecuniary society, for its morality and its ambitions. He expresses his feelings through his cynical rejection of the domestic values of a comfortable middle class, and above all through the extravagance of his consumption.

Baudelaire, who displayed great insight into the sociology of the dandy, pointed out that dandyism is the product of a transitional phase in society's evolution from an aristocracy to a democracy in which the tyranny of majority opinion reigns supreme. The dandy comes at a time which remembers enough of the old values to have a sense of style, but which acknowledges bankers and lawyers as the new élite and has no room for those who reject the pecuniary ethic.

The dandy is an outsider: declining to collaborate with the values of the society he is born into, he lacks the herd-instinct of the left, and has no peer-group, no alternative society, to confirm him in his attitudes. He is obliged to manufacture his alternative single-handed, an alternative that must be unique. He is obsessed with the quality of the statement he makes; his rejection must be displayed, his consumption conspicuous. His whole sense of identity, his very gesture of refusal, is based

44

entirely on style—a precarious, artificial creation perpetually at risk. The dandy founds his being on *cool*, which he may lose at any moment. He fights a lone battle, poised between the ridiculous and the sublime. Because ridicule will cause his immediate undoing he must always remain cold and unmoved. To be susceptible to emotion is to put his cool at risk. Consequently his eroticism lapses into Don Juanism. Pushkin's Onegin, Lermontov's Hero of our Times are classic cases in point.

Maldoror represents the ultimate in dandyism. In him its characteristics are exaggerated to an epic degree. He remains unmoved in the midst of acts of the most extreme cruelty; his self-control is never threatened. The apotheosis of total consciousness, we can never feel, as he cuts the wrist off one of his boyfriends, or passes Mervyn to the butcher, that he is at all carried away by his actions. Consider the detachment with which he contemplates the murder of Lohengrin, one of his adolescent lovers:

> For fear that he might later become like other men, I had initially decided to kill him with a knife once he passed the age of innocence. But I thought it over, and wisely I abandoned my resolve in time. He does not suspect that his life was in danger for a quarter of an hour. All was ready, and the knife had been bought. It was a pretty stiletto, for I like grace and elegance even in the instruments of death; but it was long and sharp. A single wound in the neck, carefully piercing one of the carotid arteries, and I think that would have been enough.[1]

Maldoror always acts deliberately. In this respect his portrait differs from the conventional treatment of the dandy. On the whole the dandy as portrayed in literature is finally found wanting, since his feelings have become so atrophied that he eventually proves incapable of enjoying a human relationship. Maldoror undergoes no such censure. In his case cold cerebration and reflective logic take the place of feelings as the springs of legitimate action.

He differs from his romantic predecessors in another important respect. The conventional figure of the romantic outsider conforms to a pattern first established by Milton's Satan. These archangels all fall victims to their pride, and are compelled by a heroic sense of perversity to continue their struggle against the good. Their fate is a fully justified damnation for their pursuit of evil. However we may sympathise with them, we do not doubt that they are wrong.

Not so Maldoror. For all the romantic trappings, he lacks an essential attribute of the black romantic hero: the damnation of authorial value-judgment. We can only observe his acts of rebellion, we cannot judge them. To do so would be to adopt the standpoint of judgment itself—God's values and God's viewpoint, and hence the values of the culture which Lautréamont is trying to expose. Maldoror is not judgeable, and it is this that distinguishes his acts of aggression against the 'Celestial Bandit' from romantic acts of defiance. In comparison these appear the petty tantrums of spoilt children. Maldoror represents a complete rejection of everything that God stands for. In his world it is a question of who will win, not of who is right.

The reason why Maldoror attacks God is to be found in the following passage. It describes the central vision of the entire book, an emblem that suggests that God, the fountainhead of all authority, law and sanction, may not have our well-being at heart. This view of the principle of legality echoes a sinister insight of Diderot's. He once suggested that laws are usually made for the convenience not of the citizen but of the administration. It is a vision based on just such a view of law and order that Maldoror is afforded:

[Maldoror raises his eyes] till I saw a throne made of excrement and gold, on which there reigned, with an idiot's pride, his body draped in a shroud of unwashed sick-bed sheets, the one who calls himself the Creator. He held in his hand the rotten trunk of a dead man, and raised it in turn to his eyes, his nose, his mouth; once it reached his mouth you can guess what he did with it. His feet were plunged in a vast sea of boiling blood, on its surface could be seen, appearing suddenly, like tape-worms in the contents of a chamber-pot, occasional wary heads, that vanished instantly beneath the surface, as quick as arrows: a well-directed kick on the nose being the expected reward for this infringement of regulations, occasioned by the need to breathe air, for after all these were no fish. Mere amphibians, they swam round in this filthy liquid until the Creator, finding himself empty-handed, grabbed another swimmer with the claws of his feet, as if in a vice, and raised him up in the air, out of the red slime—an exquisite sauce. He treated him as he had his predecessor. First he ate the head, legs and arms, and finally the trunk, until there was nothing left; for he crunched up the bones. And so he continued, for every hour of his eternal life. Sometimes he cried: 'I made you; therefore I may treat you as I please. You have done nothing to me, I do not deny it. I make you suffer, and it is to please me.' And he resumed his cruel meal, moving his lower jaw, which agitated his beard covered in brains. Tell me, reader, does not this final detail make your mouth water? It is not everyone who gets to eat brains like those, good fresh brains, taken from the fish-pond not a quarter of an hour ago. Paralysed, silent, I looked on for some time. Thrice I nearly fell backwards, like someone overcome with emotion; thrice I recovered. Not a nerve in my body was still; I trembled as lava trembles within a volcano. Finally my bursting lungs could no longer drive out the life-giving air fast enough, my mouth and lips opened, and I screamed, so loudly did I scream that I heard it! Suddenly the bonds were loosened from my ears, the eardrum cracked at the shock of this rushing mass of resounding air that I had spewed out with such force, and a new phenomenon came to pass in an organ that nature had condemned. I heard a sound! A fifth sense was born in me![2]

The traumatic vision of an old man with a long white beard brings Maldoror, who is anything but impassive in this instance, to his senses. It is this sudden insight into the metaphysics of law and order that creates Maldoror the militant dandy. He understands that the conventional vision we have been given of the world and our place in it is a partial vision only, that God keeps something back—the truth. Maldoror cracks the codes of his culture and thereby achieves a partial liberation from its prison. He realises that God, the *grand objet extérieur,* outside the culture-pattern and its restrictions, maintains a complete monopoly on the truth, and is impervious to anti-trust legislation. It is that realisation that motivates passages such as this:

The Eternal One has made the world as it is; he would

display great sagacity if, for exactly the time it takes to crack a woman's skull with a hammer, he would forget his astral majesty, to reveal to us the mysteries in the midst of which our existence chokes, like a fish in the bottom of a boat.[3]

Once again we find the miseries of the human condition expressed with stifling aquatic imagery.

Maldoror is determined to win for himself that portion of truth that God has kept back. In his attempt to do so he challenges Him and His creatures at every turn. The book abounds in accounts of his battles with archangels who have taken on strange forms, or, on one occasion, with Hope itself. Maldoror in the guise of an eagle fights Hope in the form of a dragon 'taller than an oak ... his whitish wings, knotted with powerful sinews, seem to have nerves of steel, so easily do they cut the air. Its body begins with a tiger's bust and ends with a long serpent's tail.' After a long and bloody combat, Maldoror tears out the dragon's heart. The episode ends as follows: 'So, Maldoror, you have conquered *Hope*! Henceforward despair will feed on the purest substance of your being. Henceforward you will walk with deliberate tread along the path of evil.'[4]

In the course of the book we witness the steady apotheosis of Maldoror until he becomes God's rival. Like Holmes and Moriarty they live in a state of uneasy truce, each one knowing that he can neither win nor be beaten.

Maldoror's ultimate ambition is to become a kind of God himself; he wants to win the lion's share. In the following passage he dreams of attaining totality, possessing the universe in an act of unnatural rape. It represents the very essence of Maldoror: a blend of aggression, homosexual eroticism, power lust and a longing for knowledge:

If only, instead of being a hell, the universe were nothing but an enormous celestial anus, observe the gesture that I make toward my loins; yes, I would force my cock through its bleeding sphincter, my impetuous movements breaking the very walls of its pelvis. Then misfortune would not have blown whole dunes of shifting sands onto my sightless eyes; I would have discovered the underground place where sleeping truth lies hidden.[5]

This is an important passage. The quality of the imagination instantly distinguishes it from the tradition of straight literature; we find nothing like it until William Burroughs. It unfolds some of the most important themes in the book. Maldoror emerges as the taboo-breaker. He assaults the very basis of culture and law, for taboo is the ultimate sanction that underwrites them. He attacks the very principle of 'Thou shalt not'. This passage tells us why.

It opens with a conditional. If this universe were not a hell in which Maldoror is blind, cut off from the truth, he would be able to possess it. He would delve into it by means of a sexual act that is taboo, censored, excluded from the conventional world-picture. But this delving remains a dream, an unrealisable hypothesis. Things being what they are, total truth, utter liberation are impossible. The author makes it clear that there is no escape. The world is as it is, and we are in it. But an understanding of our predicament, of how escape might be possible, serves to push the walls back a little. In the country of the blind it is useful to know that you have lost your sight; at least you will realise that there is more to life than the messages of your five senses.

Maldoror's mode of liberation explains one of the roles of homosexuality in this book. It represents an anti-convention, the infringement of sexual taboo. It is buggery, the incarnation of sexual taboo, grounds for irretrievable breakdown of convention, and an inappropriate subject for prose poetry, that Maldoror will employ in his bid for hidden truth. Truth and freedom will only be attained through basic transgression. This is the fundamental theme of *Les Chants*. Law and taboo are barriers erected by culture to cut its victims off from the truth. Such barriers can only be broken down by saying the unsayable, thinking the unthinkable. Lautréamont, like Nietzsche, sees the law-breaker not the law-giver as the truly creative being. For both writers the universe of the good, the universe of law is a hell in which essential truth is denied us.

Like any conscientious prophet, from Isaiah to Zarathustra, Maldoror, having gained this insight into our situation, seeks to pass his revelation on to the world. His technique is more transitive than the most violent verbal fire and brimstone. On the principle that words never hurt, Maldoror uses sticks and stones to bring man to consciousness: 'Indeed I tear away the mask from man's treacherous muddy face, and one by one ...

I cast down the sublime lies with which he deludes himself.'[6]
For 'mask' read culture, for 'lies' the principle of law and order.
Once again Nietzsche and Lautréamont are in agreement. He
too assaults humanity, suggesting that man is something to be
overcome,[7] and he sees man hiding behind the mask of culture:

> Truly, you could wear no better masks than your faces, you
> men of the present! Who could—*recognise* you?
>
> Written over with the signs of the past and these signs
> overdaubed with new signs: thus you have hidden yourselves
> well from all interpreters of signs. . . !
>
> He who tore away from you your veils and wraps and
> paint and gestures would have just enough left over to
> frighten the birds.[8]

Law-breakers like Maldoror who seek to expose the conventions that make up the mask of culture are not well received:
'This is why my hero has attracted irreconcilable hate, by
attacking man, who believed himself to be invulnerable.'[9] Man
resents Maldoror, because he resents the truth. It is weakness
that prevents him from reaching out for the liberation that
Maldoror offers. Man is appalled by Maldoror and rejects him
out of hand, but perhaps it is only his self-deluding hypocrisy
that prevents him from seeing that he has more in common
with Maldoror than he would care to think: '[The poet] does
not claim that his warblings are totally unfamiliar: on the
contrary he congratulates himself with the thought that the
lofty and wicked ideas of his hero are to be found in all men.'[10]
The difference between Maldoror and other men is that he is
able to face up to himself, where others have to hide from each
other and themselves behind their cultural masks: 'He then
perceived that he was born wicked: extraordinary blow of fate
. . . he admitted the truth and said that he was cruel . . . Did
you hear him, mankind? He dares to say it with this trembling
pen!'[11] He writes not for public acclaim but in order to 'Paint the
joys of cruelty. Delights neither transitory nor artificial . . .
because you are cruel, does it mean that you cannot have
genius?'[12]

Maldoror is not content with admitting the truth about himself. He also wishes to instruct us in unpalatable truths. His
purpose is educational, and if the education does us violence no

matter; Maldoror would be the first to agree that to spare the rod is to spoil the child. Man believed that:

he was composed only of good and a minimal quantity of evil. Abruptly I showed him, by exposing his heart, his intrigues, that on the contrary he is composed of evil with a minimal quantity of good, which the legislators have the greatest difficulty in preserving from evaporation.[13]

Because man will neither believe nor accept the truth about himself, psychology is still in its infancy:

Man hypocritically says yes and thinks no. This is why the pigs of humanity have such trust in one another and are not selfish. Psychology still has a long way to go.[14]

In forcing man's attention on his instinctive love of cruelty, no less real for being inadmissible, Maldoror appeals to man's repressed and secret self. Desires that normally have to be sublimated by culture into notions such as crime and punishment, law-enforcement, the obscene rituals of social justice and authoritarianism, are exposed by Maldoror for what they are: institutions created by society to permit its leaders to exercise their natural, instinctive desire to treat their fellows as their slaves, without abdicating from their role as do-gooders and pillars of the community: to behave, in short, like miniature versions of the eating God. Social man may revolt at what Maldoror has to say, but social man's *id* reacts as follows:

Reader, perhaps it is hate that you wish me to invoke at the beginning of this work. Who is to say that you will not, bathed in countless sensual pleasures, sniff to your heart's content with your wide thin conceited nostrils, turning up your belly like a shark in the fine black air, as if you understood the importance of this action, and the no less great importance of your legitimate appetite, breathing in the red scent slowly and majestically. Believe me, it will gladden the two shapeless holes of your vile muzzle, oh monster.[15]

The author of *Les Chants* suggests that we are being hypocritical if we pronounce ourselves disgusted by his poetry, with a hypocrisy that is fundamental to human nature. In Plato's *Republic* Socrates recounts an incident that illustrates the indignation and reluctance which we feel when obliged to acknowledge this side of ourselves:

Leontion, son of Aglaion, was on his way up from Piraeus, outside the north wall, when he noticed some corpses lying on the ground with the executioner standing beside them. He wanted to go and look at them, and yet at the same time he held himself back in disgust. For a time he struggled with himself and averted his eyes, but in the end his desire got the better of him and he ran up to the corpses, opening his eyes and saying to them, 'There you are, curse you—a lovely sight! Have a real good look.'[16]

Maldoror invites *us* to take a look, knowing that, secretly, we are curious. If we profess to find it all too disgusting, we deceive ourselves. We reject, in one form, attitudes and relationships that society encourages us to adopt in others. These are simply more effective in their reconciliation of our desires with our delusions. There are those of us who may be moved by the fall of a sparrow but who scarcely blink as another Indian bites the dust. As Maldoror points out, if one wishes to enjoy the pleasures of killing with impunity, one simply has to practise murder wholesale: 'You see that when you wish to become famous, you must plunge gracefully into rivers of blood, fed by cannon fodder.'[17]

Passages such as this demonstrate that one of the functions of *Les Chants* is to force us to face the unpalatable truths that are usually obscured by cultural overlay. We are all cruel, but most of us prefer not to admit it. It is *we* who are responsible for the naked horror of the work: its hero Maldoror is exceptional in his honesty, not in his morals. As Gogol writes in the epigraph to *The Inspector General*, 'Don't blame the mirror if you see an ugly face.' Still less should we blame Maldoror, for it is not his face that we see in the mirror; it is his hand that we can feel holding us by the scruff of the neck and forcing us to look.

Maldoror's dandyism reflects an attitude of fundamental refusal. He rejects the world of culture as a world of partial truth, designed in the first instance to conceal from mankind his actual situation as victim of the eating God, secondly to permit men to reconcile their instinctive love of cruelty with their desire to approve of themselves. Maldoror's aggression is designed to bring us to consciousness, compelling us to see the world as it really is.

PART TWO

Les Chants de Maldoror

CHAPTER SIX

Black Humour and the Absurd

The most striking literary quality of *Les Chants* is the depth and range of its black humour. The book reads like a sustained sick joke, the work of an author who is not laughing. Lautréamont's cruelty is cruelty without sentiment—the cruelty of black humour. Maldoror's actions are refrigerated, they numb our consciousness with the anaesthetic of ritual. His world is formalised in such a way that victim and executioner have no alternative but to play their parts. Witness the account of a shipwreck in which Maldoror ensures that no one escapes—out of a sense of pure obligation:

> They could not escape! As an additional precaution, I had fetched my double-barrelled gun, so that, should some ship-wrecked sailor try to swim to the rocks, to escape imminent death, a bullet in the shoulder might break his arm and thwart his design. At the very height of the storm, I saw, swimming through the water, with desperate efforts, a determined head, with streaming hair. He was swallowing litres of water, plunging into the abyss, tossed like a cork. Only to reappear, hair streaming; fastening his eye on the shore, he seemed to defy death. His *sang-froid* was admirable. A large and bloody wound, inflicted by some hidden rock, scarred his noble and intrepid face. He could have been no more than sixteen, for one could just make out by the lightning the peach-like down on his lip. Now he was no more than two hundred metres from the cliff; I could easily see him. What courage! What boundless spirit! How his steadfast head seemed to defy destiny, as it cut vigorously through the waves, their furrows opening with difficulty before him . . . My mind was made up. I owed it to myself to keep my promise: the last hour had struck for one and all, none must escape. That was my decision; nothing would change it. A crisp report was heard, and the head went under

at once, never to reappear. I did not enjoy that murder as much as you might think; it was precisely because I was glutted with perpetual killing that I carried on, a habit I could not forgo, but which only gave the slightest of pleasures.[1]

This ritualistic conception of the aesthetics of cruelty is a direct anticipation of Antonin Artaud's *Theatre of Cruelty*. He too sees in it the basis of a new art form. He wishes to restore the theatre to its essential role as a place of savagery and magic—a theatre of ritual. Western Society had trivialised drama, and Artaud sought to revive its primitive force; to create a world as remote as possible from the wit of Anouilh and Giraudoux, a savage, ritualistic world of visceral cries and archetypal gestures, a world very close to Lautréamont.

Artaud saw poetry as a process of radicalisation, a means of breaking down our conventional mental sets, or, in our terms, of smashing the grid. He wants us to re-think from first principles:

Poetry is anarchic in that it questions all relationships between object and object, form and meaning. It is anarchic also in so far as it exists as the result of a disorder that brings us nearer to on chaos.[2]

The mainspring of the new poetry will be cruelty. This does not necessarily mean sheer violence. It is a new order, a strange ice-cold ritual:

It is a mistake to impart to the word cruelty the sense of a bloody discipline, the gratuitous and disinterested searching-out of physical pain and evil. The Ethiopian chief, who drives conquered princes before him and enslaves them, does not do so out of a desperate blood-lust. In fact cruelty does not mean blood, martyred flesh, crucified enemies. This equation of cruelty with torture is a side-issue. Cruelty has a kind of higher order, which governs the executioner himself, and to which he must be *determined* to submit if necessary. Above all cruelty is lucid, it is a kind of inflexible directive, a submission to necessity. There is no cruelty without consciousness, without a kind of applied consciousness. It is a consciousness that gives its tinge of blood, its hint of cruelty to every act of life, because of course life is always somebody else's death.[3]

To achieve such cruelty Lautréamont employs black humour. As a one-sided way of handling a situation, it serves his purpose admirably. Never taking account of the feeling tone of victim or criminal it bleeds all situations of emotion and turns everything into automated ritual.

As we roar with laughter at the sight of an old gentleman slipping on a banana skin, we never think that he may have broken his back. The business of black humour is to re-write human tragedy in terms of slipping on a banana skin. It reduces its protagonists to puppets, automata that lack the full emotional range of humanity. As Maldoror swings Mervyn against the parapet, we smile: Maldoror is so vile, Mervyn so well-mannered, that the passage is unaccountably funny.

Black humour may best be thought of as the language of super-irony. It has the effect of irony, multiplied a thousandfold, of rendering what it describes distanced and remote. For example, when Maldoror contemplates the torture of some luckless youth, the tone is so hysterical that it is camp. An alienating effect sets in and what appeared at first sight to be written in the heat of passion suddenly seems as cold as ice:

One must let one's nails grow a fortnight. Oh the joy of snatching brutally from his bed a child who still has no down on his upper lip. With wide open eyes you pretend to pass your hand gently across his brow, sweeping back his beautiful hair. Then, suddenly, when he least expects it, you plunge your long nails into his soft chest, but without killing him; for if he were to die you would not be able to witness his suffering later. Then, you drink his blood, licking his wounds; and all this time, which should last an eternity, the child weeps. Nothing tastes as good as his blood, drawn from him in the manner described, still warm, unless it be his tears, bitter as salt ... Bandage his eyes as you tear his quivering flesh; and, when you have listened for hours to his sublime cries ... rush in from the next room, as if to come to his rescue. Untie his hands with their swollen veins and sinews, restore sight to his wild staring eyes, and once more begin to lick his tears and blood. How genuine is your repentance!

The divine spark within us, that appears so seldom, comes too late.[4]

The torturer proceeds to console his victim, according himself the best of both worlds.

Black humour and cruelty are taken a stage further in a passage in which Maldoror addresses an innocent young girl who appears to love him:

> I might take your head in my hands, as if in a gentle caress, only to plunge my avid fingers into the lobes of your innocent brain, in order to extract from it, smiling, a healing grease to soothe my eyes, aching from the eternal insomnia of life. I might stitch up your eyelids with a needle, depriving you of the sight of the universe, rendering you unable to find your way; I would not be the one to guide you.[5]

The world of black humour is exaggerated, hysterical and more than a little implausible. The following episode combines cruelty and absurdity to create one of the blackest, most disturbing passages in Western literature. A demented mother tells the story of Maldoror's meeting with her daughter:

> Maldoror was passing by with his bulldog: he saw a girl sleeping under a plane tree; and at first he mistook her for a rose ... He undressed quickly, like a man who knew what he was about. Naked as a stone, he threw himself on the body of the girl and raised her dress to commit an act of gross indecency ... by daylight! Of course he was not ashamed. Let us not dwell upon this impure deed. Dissatisfied, he dressed again quickly, glanced prudently down the dusty road, saw no one, and ordered his bulldog to strangle the blood-stained girl with the movement of his jaws. He showed the mountain dog the spot where the suffering victim breathed and screamed, and stepped aside in order to avoid seeing how the sharp teeth slip into the rosy veins. The bulldog found his orders somewhat severe. He believed that he had to do what had already been done, and the wolf of the monstrous muzzle was simply content, in his turn, to ravish the virginity of this delicate creature. Once more blood flowed from her torn person, down her legs and across the meadow. Her groans mingled with the animal's whimpers.

The girl offered him the gold cross that hung about her neck, begging him to spare her; she had not dared to offer it to the fierce gaze of him who first thought to exploit the frailty of her youth. But the dog well knew that if he disobeyed his master, a knife thrown from his sleeve would suddenly split open his guts, without warning. Maldoror (how I hate to pronounce that name!) heard the cries of pain and was surprised that the victim took so long to die. He approached the sacrificial altar, and observed his bulldog indulging in lewd practices, raising his head over the young girl, as a shipwrecked mariner raises his head above the angry billows. He gave him a kick and split an eye. The bulldog ran off in a rage, dragging with him for a short distance that seemed long, however short it might have been, the girl's dangling body, which only came away as a consequence of the jerky movements of his flight; but he feared to attack the master whom he was to see no more. The latter took from his pocket an American pen-knife, with ten or twelve blades that had various uses. He opened the angular legs of this steel Hydra; and equipped with this scalpel, seeing that the grass had not yet disappeared beneath so great a flow of blood, he prepared, without blenching, bravely to explore the wretched child's vagina. From this enlarged orifice he extracted a series of organs; intestines, lungs, liver and finally the heart itself were removed from their foundations and dragged out into the light of day through the horrid opening. The torturer perceived that the girl, like a drawn chicken, had been dead for some time.[6]

We are obliged to treat this as black humour, cling to the funny side, out of sheer self-defence. The alternative,. to let it appeal to our sense of compassion, would produce a reaction of quite intolerable intensity.

In passages such as these Lautréamont uses our sense of revulsion as a source of humour. The sheer strength of the writing, its capacity to shock, and our capacity to be shocked, is treated as a source of mind-expanding amusement. Since it is merely an intensification of the familiar literature of romantic agony, it makes us re-think our attitudes to romantic rhetoric. In that respect Lautréamont's writing can teach us things about ourselves, making us analyse our disgust, and find beneath it perhaps not revulsion alone, but a compound of fear and fascination. The distancing effect of black humour helps us to feel detached about the most unlikely subjects and situations, thereby helping us to acquire some of that self-knowledge that Lautréamont is trying to impart to his readers.

It is obvious that black humour cannot rely on subject-matter alone to achieve its particular effect. It would be quite possible to describe the gentleman slipping on a banana skin in terms that would inspire pity rather than laughter. Black humour is utterly dependent on tone. It requires a blend of deadpan detachment and immaculate sense of timing. It is admirably characterised by the French equivalent for deadpan humour: *pince-sans-rire*. *Les Chants* pinch on every page.

The author describes the most unpleasant incidents with an irreverent flippancy. Maldoror wounds an archangel by licking its cheek:

> Look, just look at that pink and white cheek turned black as coal. It stinks. Gangrene. No question of it.[7]

In similar style he describes the habits and physical characteristics of dogs:

> Woe betide the tardy traveller! The haunters of cemeteries will throw themselves upon him, will rend him, eat him with their bloody mouths; for there is nothing wrong with their teeth.[8]

Elsewhere he describes a corpse that Maldoror has hurled against a wall:

> Doubtless the corpse remained splattered against the wall, like a ripe pear, and did not fall to the ground; but dogs can jump high, if you don't watch out.[9]

Lautréamont relies on stylistic incongruity for comic effects. He will describe actions with an absurdly meticulous care. Care and detail suggest restraint, emotional detachment, the attitude of the scientific observer, rather than the feeling tone of the protagonist. The incongruous marriage of tone and topic provides for a source of ironic humour in passages such as this,

where Maldoror addresses God, who has just struck him with a
thunderbolt. Maldoror seems unconcerned:

> Moreover, you felt it appropriate to your majesty, after due
> reflection, to draw from my forehead a cup of blood![10]

The tone is utterly inappropriate to the description of violent
action. Incongruity becomes a comic device. The reader feels
that the author cannot be serious if he writes so flippantly of
such dreadful events. He is not being serious, he is being funny.
Here is the ludicrous story of how Maldoror tried to laugh:

> All my life, I have seen men with narrow shoulders perform
> stupid and numerous actions, brutalise their fellows, cor-
> rupting souls by every possible means. They call the motives
> of their actions glory. When I saw such spectacles I wished to
> laugh, as other men; but, curious imitation, it was not pos-
> sible. I took a pen-knife with a sharp blade, and split my
> flesh at the spot where the lips join. For a moment I believed
> I had achieved my goal. I observed that mouth damaged by
> my own hand in the glass! I was wrong! Moreover the
> blood that flowed so freely from my two wounds prevented
> me from seeing whether or not it was really a laugh like that
> of others. But, after a few moments comparison, I soon saw
> that my laugh did not resemble a human laugh, that is to say
> that I was not laughing.[11]

Scenes such as these, described in the pompous and inappropriate language that Lautréamont adopts, do not feel
right. They are strangely incomplete, lacking the essential
human ingredient of a sense of emotion. Artaud talks of the
determinism of cruelty. It is the same ritualistic inevitability
that regulates the world of Maldoror, a world so ordered that
there is no place for pity or humanity. Black humour turns
everything it touches into a strangely stylised two-dimensional
distortion: a conventionalised rendering of a cartoon world
in which Maldoror rapes and murders his way through some
demented Disneyland.

Lautréamont seems to be using black humour as he did the
novel, to draw our attention to the secret under-belly of the
culture-pattern. He uses the language of the establishment, the
pompous French of academics, academicians and political

figures, to describe scenes of unparalleled violence and obscenity. The style may seem inappropriate, but perhaps that impropriety is only skin-deep? Perhaps the style our culture uses to express itself on its most solemn occasions is the proper style to describe the violently obscene dream-life of a society founded on aggression.

More technical reasons may also have encouraged Lautréamont in his choice of style. Stylistic incongruity draws attention to the relationship between rhetoric and reality, between a sign and what it refers to (its referent). By creating an inappropriate marriage of sign and referent the author encourages us to question the propriety of more regular relationships. As an author, he is free to describe an event in any style he chooses. His choice of style is in no sense determined by any element of non-linguistic reality. There is nothing more 'real' about one type of sign than there is about another. Lautréamont, by his use of incongruity, makes us grasp this essential truth, which leads in turn to the realisation that culture itself is the mere product of convention; no more than the sum of its signs.

Black humour in the hands of Lautréamont acts as a means of linguistic alienation—taking that word in the Brechtian sense of 'making strange'. It is its alienating capacity that makes black humour a primary element in the most important artistic code of our age: the code of the absurd.

Writers such as Camus and Ionesco seek to describe human behaviour in a way that takes it out of the context of everyday reality, in which we accept it without question. Re-situating human action in situations that are provocatively unfamiliar, they present it in such a way that we are made to realise that the behaviour patterns we took for granted as rational and meaningful are usually empty habits void of all meaning.

The literature of the absurd is an art form generated by a society at odds with itself. Its practitioners express a refusal to be regulated by the conventions, categories and prescriptions of their culture-pattern. Their art expresses a vote of no confidence in the official guide.

No wonder that Lautréamont makes ample use of the absurd. His work is studded with gems of absurdity and pseudo-logic such as the following account of the last moments of some drowning sailors:

Each one tells himself that once in the water, he will be unable to breathe; for, as far back as he can remember, he acknowledges no fish in his family tree; but he urges himself to hold his breath for as long as he can, in order to prolong his life for two or three seconds.[12]

The author has chosen to make the events appear ridiculous, but he could equally well have made them poignant, for language is a mirror that can distort reality according to the whim of its user.

One of Lautréamont's stranger whims might be termed the aesthetic of the bad joke. One of the characteristics of the humour of the absurd is that jokes do not need to be funny to succeed as jokes, just very sick. It can use the most excruciating puns, and their very badness appears to act in their favour. Black humour is the genre in which you get away with murder. This is because in both the moral and the photographic sense, it projects a negative world-view. Everything is in reverse, all rules are inverted: here deliberately and perversely unfunny jokes become the funniest of all. Hence the impact of peculiarly feeble jokes such as the sailors' discovery that they have no fish in their pedigree. The author makes such comments carefully. There can be no question of explaining such jokes away as a lapse of taste or a slip of the pen. He is writing about a world in which all taste has long since lapsed, and if we are ready to explain away one bad joke as a slip of the pen, we will soon find ourselves dismissing the entire work as a slip of the mind. He must know what he is doing when he writes lines such as:

Forgive me, I had the impression that my hair was standing on end; but it was nothing, I had no difficulty in putting it back into place with my hand.[13]

These passages are meant not seriously, but absurdly. The absurd consists, in his own words, of 'the serious appearance of that which is really only grotesque'.[14] He warns us that 'it will often happen that I shall utter the most preposterous propositions in solemn tones'.[15]

His use of the absurd is another invitation to think about the relationship between artistic conventions and the real world, about the nature of media-distortion. It is, sadly enough, all too possible to illustrate Lautréamont's last statement with examples taken from the news media, and their capacity to create non-events: a trivial incident is given all the merciless, hard-hitting probing that we have come to expect from the television journalist who acts as the keeper of the public conscience. His end-product may have all the appearance of a story, all the rhetorical qualities associated with earth-shattering news, yet nothing has actually taken place.

It is too easy to assume that media and subject, word and object, enjoy a necessary relationship. The art of the absurd, making the greatest possible use of aesthetic incongruity, serves as a reminder that the relationship is one of pure convention— that the media are not real.

This is why *Les Chants* makes extravagant use of incongruity, to create a topsy-turvy *Through The Looking-Glass* world. On one occasion Maldoror is visited by his conscience, who has descended to earth in order to urge him to reform. It delivers an impassioned speech that might have come straight from *Pinocchio*, but its high seriousness is somewhat marred by the fact that Maldoror's conscience has appeared in the form of a toad. Toad takes his leave :

And now farewell; do not expect the toad to cross your path again. You were the cause of my death. I depart for eternity, in order to beg that you be forgiven.[16]

Animals provide the author with widely varied sources of absurdity. He places them in inappropriate contexts: 'Neither I, nor the four webbed feet of the polar bear, have been able to discover the secret of life.'[17] He uses them to arrive at pseudo-logical conclusions that are no less disturbing for making sense: 'The elephant lets you caress it. The louse doesn't.'[18] There may be more regular ways of telling elephants from lice, but this does not invalidate Lautréamont's method. He never permits his taxonomies to be affected by considerations of size. Size alone never keeps species apart: 'Indeed we are allowed to kill flies and even rhinoceroses.'[19] This is a singular piece of absurdity. Superficially resembling the preceding examples, it has another layer of meaning, in that it anticipates the final downfall of God in rhinoceros guise.

Lautréamont understands that cocks cannot read, but he has

his own explanation: 'The cock remains true to its nature ...
Teach it to read and it revolts. It is no parrot.'[20] Elsewhere he
refers to the philosopher who laughed at the sight of a donkey
eating a fig. He inverts the proposition and goes one better:
'I saw a fig eat a donkey! But I did not laugh.'[21]

We see here the humour of the absurd at work. Where
practical jokes manipulate elements of reality such as old men
and banana skins, the absurd manipulates not reality, but the
signs that provide a conventionalised rendering of that reality.
The absurd is based on the aesthetic of the impractical joke.

Our symbol systems, numbers, letters, can be assembled in
such a way that they create models that reflect reality more or
less adequately. The humour of the absurd uses the fact that
these systems are not restricted to the exclusive representation of
the real and the possible. As open-ended systems that can adapt
to all the vicissitudes of reality, and are consequently extraordinarily flexible, it happens that they are equally adaptable
to the representation of that which is not possible at all. They
can be used to write nonsense, the square root of minus one.
There is nothing in the rules for the system, in this case the
syntax of standard French (in the conventional, as opposed to
the Chomskian, sense), that makes the statement 'Une figue
mange un âne' any less possible to generate than the statement
'Un âne mange une figue'. Practitioners of the absurd exploit this
lack of discrimination between what makes sense to the system
and what makes sense to the world. They use the rules of the
system to create an infinity of parallel para-logical worlds,
which are not chaotic, but governed by sets of rules that
happen not to be our own.

CHAPTER SEVEN

The Ideology of the Absurd

It is above all Lautréamont's extensive use of black humour and the absurd that makes him important today. The most significant feature of twentieth-century art is its rejection of the straight world-view, and the artist's refusal to accept the culture passed on to him by his own particular *ancien régime*.

In the arts, the establishment view comes across as 'realism'. This was the only tenable attitude, the only one to withstand the acid test of common sense. Realism generated the empirical three-dimensional space created, on the visual plane, by the invention of vanishing-point perspective in the painting of the High Renaissance, and on the philosophical plane by the empiricism and scepticism of Bacon and Montaigne.

In the course of this century that picture has been recognised as culture-bound: the product of a particular civilisation, practical, mercantile, secular, linear and profit-motivated—the culture of the straight society. That such a view has strict limitations is one of the truths that the post-McLuhan generation hold to be self-evident. But to their immediate predecessors the discovery came as something of a shock. In the 1970s we are attuned to change and surprised by stability— hence our sentimental affection for the unchanging and stable folkways of primitive cultures—but as late as the 1920s European culture still thought of stability as its natural state. The first contact that the *avant-garde* made with an accelerating rate of change had a traumatic impact:

> We are living in an age that is probably unique in the history of the world, a time when the world . . . is seeing its old values collapse. Life, burnt to a cinder, is falling away, crumbling. On the moral or social plane this comes out as a monstrous unleashing of appetites, a release of the base instincts, the crackling of burnt-up lives, prematurely exposed to the flame.

What is interesting about these events today is not the events

66

themselves, but this moral boiling-point at which they maintain our minds; this extreme degree of tension. It is a state of conscious chaos into which they plunge us without cease.[1]

In its most acute form this shock accounts not only for Artaud's *Theatre of Cruelty*, but for the entire literature of the absurd. From Voltaire through the romantics to Kafka, the surrealists, Camus, down to Burroughs and Joseph Heller, we witness the gradual evolution of an awareness of the limitations of the conventional view of reality. There is a growing sense of the lack of relationship between realism and reality, a tendency to portray the world in a way that reduces the codes of realism to a nonsense. In *Catch-22* Major Cathcart asks Yossarian, who refuses to fly any more missions in case he gets killed, what would happen if everyone felt that way. 'I'd be a fool to feel any different,' comes the answer. A logical answer, reminiscent of the French army in 1940, but unrealistic and hence absurd.

The literature of the absurd is essentially a protest literature: the reflection of a refusal to play the game by the old rules because the old rules no longer work. It challenges and rejects the conventional view of reality, but not for the sheer joy of the challenge, which is a game best left to philosophers and metaphysicians. Such challenges only begin to matter when the world-view in question is felt to require negation because it no longer satisfies man's sense of what is good, true and beautiful.

Realism is the product of a self-satisfied culture, one that likes itself enough to enjoy art forms that hold up a mirror to it. The tradition of the portrait as a major art form dates, significantly, from the Renaissance paintings of popes and patrons, and culminates in Ingres' superb renderings of luminaries of the July Monarchy such as the banker Bertin and the Baroness de Rothschild.

Surrealism and the literature of the absurd are the products of a culture at odds with itself. It is no coincidence that absurdity comes into its own in the years following the First World War, that one of its greatest heroes should be the incomparable Schweik. It is an aesthetic language specially designed to deal with disaster on a colossal scale, and war features regularly as its major subject.

The aesthetics of the absurd first play an important part in

Voltaire's *Candide*, the first work in modern times to employ black humour as its literary staple.

Candide describes the world of the Seven Years War, colonialism, natural disaster and the Inquisition. The comedy derives from the naive expectations of Candide, who believes himself to be in the best of all possible worlds. He expects virtue to be rewarded, vice chastised, and justice to reign supreme. Above all he expects his world to be ordered; for there to be an overriding, necessary, ethical relationship between events, and the universe to be governed by a principle of benevolent cause and effect. But Candide's world is not like that. It offers an absurd and haphazard succession of events in which vice is rewarded, virtue chastised and Candide is reunited with his long-lost love Cunégonde, only to discover that she has become hideously ugly and a shrew to boot.

Voltaire suggests that things are not as our picture of an ordered universe would have them. Our conventional world-view will always disappoint because we live in a world that is cruel, disordered and void of meaning.

In order to make his point Voltaire's narrative surprises at every turn. He perpetually creates expectations in his reader, and then, with the most exquisite sense of timing, it is the very opposite that comes about. Voltaire writes of a world that is littered with banana skins, and his hero slips on every one. But he never expects to fall; when he goes down for the fiftieth time he is as surprised as ever.

The author uses all the distancing qualities of black humour. We have no feeling for his characters because they are portrayed in a one-sided way: puppets moving jerkily through their pre-determined movements. We never respond to them fully, they resemble the comics of silent movies, going through their slapstick routines with immaculate timing, but so portrayed that we never feel that they hurt themselves as they fall downstairs. They invariably bounce up and move off, ready to tumble down another flight.

Through this aesthetic language Voltaire voices the awful suspicion that we live in a world without order or meaning, both arbitrary and absurd. This suspicion that reality is not what it appears is developed by the romantics, notably by Gogol. He is haunted by the belief that reality may be only skin-deep, that at any moment it may melt away to reveal the devil knows what. His *St Petersburg Stories* deal with the erosion of reality by the forces of disorder. St Petersburg is the unreal soulless city inhabited by zombies, a place in which you can be sure of nothing. You cannot even be sure of your own face: witness the fate of the luckless Kovalev in *The Nose*. He awakes one morning to find his nose is missing. He goes out in search of it and sees it stepping into a carriage, dressed as a civil servant of rank. In St Petersburg the air of reality is so thin that anything can happen.

The encroachment of the unknown is even more pronounced in the work of Kafka. What began with Voltaire as an uneasy suspicion has become a matter of fact. In Kafka's world you are quite likely to be on trial for your life, on an unspecified charge. Punishment may involve metamorphosis into an insect, or incarceration in a penal settlement where a machine will carve an account of your offence upon your back—always provided that it does not go wrong and cut you to ribbons.

By the time of William Burroughs encroachment has reached hysteria. He offers an interesting set of permutations on fates worse than death; they include arrest at the hands of a junk-shooting narcotics squad, and having the reality sucked out of you by an inter-galactic advertising agency just as your planet goes nova.

From *Candide* to *The Naked Lunch* there develops a pattern of satire and rejection of a world that, absurd though it may be, nonetheless presents a terrible threat. Around each corner you may meet Ubu Roi, who will stick small pieces of wood into your ears, feed you to his machine for the extraction of brain and then realise his ultimate threat: 'I'll kill everybody and then I'll go away.'

It is Alfred Jarry who is closest of all to the tone and feeling of *Les Chants*. Both writers have a love of cold, mathematical precision. Neither laughs as he tells his hair-raising jokes. They both describe a world of feelingless violence, that is unaccountably hilarious. Jarry's principal creation, Ubu, is one of the great grotesques of our civilization. He is a totally one-sided character, all appetite and id. He pays no lip-service to the reality principle and is concerned solely with his own pleasure and the accumulation of *phynance*. He is not capable of positive emotion; his reaction to someone who saves his life is to hit him over the head when he's not looking, in case he has money in his pocket. In Ubu self-interest is enlarged to super-human proportions. A colossus of appetite dwarfing even Maldoror, he is also a coward. He has not a single redeeming feature. Pure monster, he robs and murders his way through a farcical world. As Jarry writes in a stage direction to *Ubu Roi*: 'The action takes place in Poland, that is to say nowhere.' Like Maldoror's, the world of Ubu is strangely mechanised. Its mechanical qualities are embodied in his machine for the extraction of brain, and even more so in his three henchmen. The *palotins* are violent, feelingless robots, half man, half machine. Their one delight is to impale Ubu's enemies—and anyone else who may be in the offing. They are a terrible surrealistic Gestapo.

Ubu treats his conscience even more cavalierly than does Maldoror: it spends most of its time locked up in a suitcase where it can do no harm. Ubu is in every way as violent as Maldoror, the only difference being that he is presented entirely through the code of farce. Maldoror's violence is less abstract, allowed to appear a little closer to home.

Even more than Lautréamont, Jarry employs the techniques and possibilities of the absurd. In *Ubu Enchaîné* we find ourselves in a free country: when drilling troops you must order a left turn when you want them to turn right, and Ubu discovers that a slave is the freest man of all.

Jarry follows Lautréamont in his use of utterly incongruous language in order to render the familiar strange. It is on this basis that he writes a *Passion of Christ Considered as an Uphill Bicycle Race*. He uses the same method on a more modest scale to describe the business of posting a letter.

The New Stamps

A human superstition suggests that when you wish to communicate with friends, temporarily absent, you toss into openings that, in this respect, resemble the mouths of drains, the written expression of your feelings, after having propitiated the tobacco trade with some offering ... and received in exchange some tiny images, no doubt blessed, which you kiss devoutly on the rear. This is not the place to criticise the absurdity of these actions; there is no doubt that they render long-distance communication possible.[2]

Jarry gives a name to his science: 'Pataphysics', the study of imaginary solutions obtaining in universes parallel to our own. It represents the elaborate and careful construction of a kind of non-Euclidean world-view. There is no doubt whatsoever that Lautréamont was a pataphysician *avant la lettre*.

This kind of fantastic speculation comes across as something more than pretty whimsy, and Lewis Carroll penetrates deeper and is psychically more relevant than Tolkien, because we can no longer be quite certain of the media-saturated environment in which we live. It may look real enough, but so does the TV newscaster. It comes as something of a shock to discover that, like an actor, the newscaster wears make-up. Where does his acting stop?

As what passes for reality is steadily eroded by commercial and political dream-machines, and our loss of confidence in that reality increases accordingly, we have more and more need of the parallel worlds of writers such as Lautréamont and Jarry. These worlds are at least consistent, not unlike our own in some respects, and are supported by an authenticity utterly lacking in our own snap-crackle-pop environment—the authenticity of the imagination. There is nothing facile about Lautréamont's dream-life, nothing *ersatz* about his fantasies. At least *their reality* is not in doubt.

The imaginative writer J. G. Ballard, whose own work has intense imaginative authenticity, finds in surrealism and its ancestors Jarry and Lautréamont a means of resisting the steady erosion of our sense of reality by the media:

The techniques of surrealism have a particular relevance at this moment, when the fictional elements in the world around us are multiplying to the point where it is almost impossible to distinguish between the 'real' and the 'false'—the terms no longer have any meaning. The faces of public figures are projected at us as if out of some endless global pantomime, they and the events in the world at large have the conviction and reality of those depicted on giant advertisement hoardings. The task of the arts seems more and more to be that of isolating the few elements of reality from this

71

mélange of fictions, not some metaphorical 'reality', but simply the basic elements of cognition and posture that are the jigs and props of our consciousness.[3]

Black humour and the absurd play such an important role in contemporary culture for another, tactical, reason. As literary modes they are associated with disaster. They have nothing to do with the language of happiness. They have become the prime medium with which to render a negative view of the world and, in this respect, they have supplanted other modes that fulfilled that function in the past.

If we date the rise of black humour from *Candide* (1759), we find that earlier generations used two forms to express a negative world view: tragedy and Christian homily. If we can see how these differ from black comedy in scope and strategy, we may understand the particular qualities that black humour has to offer.

Christian apology, as represented, for example, by the writing of Pascal, expresses the most pessimistic view of the world. Man is a helpless creature beset by disasters on every side. The world is a prison, a vale of tears, and we, the prisoners, are perpetually at each others' throats. Pascal's picture is relieved by two interlocking mitigating factors. Man is saved from total brutishness by his spirituality. He may be a reed, but he is a thinking reed. Pascal offers a kind of hope in his belief in man's ability to transcend himself. The second factor is of course much more important: Christian apology of the Pascalian kind describes the world as a vale of tears, but sets against this the joys of paradise to come. 'Now may be bad, but later . . .'

This picture has two functions. The first is obvious—the proselytising one, a before and after hard sell. It is the second that is the more important for our purpose. Promise of salvation acts, in sociological terms, as an effective means of reconciling one to the unrelieved horror of the present. The knowledge that all this is only temporary, a form of purgatory to be crowned with an eternal golden future, helps us tolerate an otherwise intolerable present.

There is a certain parallel between this kind of promise and the promise of the weekly lottery. Betting on a hundred-thousand-to-one long shot is a mug's game for a gambler. But as a way of financing a dream it is extraordinarily effective. For a small weekly investment you buy a stake in a hope that makes ghetto life more tolerable. It is something very close to the Pascalian argument, considered from the viewpoint not of its meaning, but of its sociological use.

Tragedy has a similar role. It too sets out to reconcile its public with disaster. It portrays a series of appalling events in the lives of people in enviable social situations. It can already be seen to have a euphemising function. It tells its audience, which was certainly not made up exclusively of royalty and nobility in the sixteenth and seventeenth centuries, that life is tough at the top. This reconciles the average under-privileged commoner with the reality of his social situation. At the same time, by taking kings and queens as its protagonists, it deals with the very lynch-pins of its society, and thereby takes on a general social significance.

More important than the status of the characters is the nature of the disasters that befall them. Tragedy seeks to persuade us that the horrendous events it describes happened with good reason. Aristotle states that if a statue were to fall on and kill a passer-by, this would be tragedy only if it were the statue of someone he had murdered. This points to the function of tragedy, which is not to purge fear and pity, but to persuade its audience of the propriety of terror.

Tragic victims may not be responsible for their fate in any obvious way, and yet we are made to feel that, in some strange sense, they get their deserts. Hence the importance of the 'tragic flaw'. As Gloucester has his eyes put out, or Hippolytus is torn apart, we accept these fates as appropriate. Our sense of propriety expresses itself in catharsis; we are relieved of our fear and our pity because the play suggests that some kind of justice has been done. We come to feel that incest, parricide, even the destruction of innocence, are part of a design, that we live in a universe with a purpose, one in which it is right that Hamlet should die, appropriate for Oedipus to punish his eyes with a golden pin, in atonement for a case of mistaken identity. *As flies to wanton boys, are we to the gods: they kill us for their sport,* but at least there are gods, and we know the name of the game.

A sense of order is quite essential to tragedy. We must feel that we are witnessing the enactment of a ritual pattern from which there can be no departure. The protagonists have no choice, they can neither change the rules nor decline to play. The inevitable pattern that is imposed upon the tragic hero is made the subject of the first of the poems of Yuri Zhivago. 'Hamlet' makes it bitterly clear that Zhivago has no choice:

> But the order of the acts is predetermined
> And the end of the road cannot be avoided
> I am alone, it all collapses into phariseeism
> To live your life out—is not to cross a field.

Along with its sense of order tragedy has a second important feature—its restricted focus. However terrible the events it portrays, its form contains them. The shape of the play, the pattern of the verse, set up lines of force that control the events, shaping them into a meaningful pattern. Disaster becomes something essentially limited, something that may, in the final analysis, be transcended.

This element of control is an essential part of the tragic experience. Without it, one could not achieve the strange sense of uplift that one feels at the end of *Hamlet* or *Phèdre*; that sense of muted exaltation that dawns on us with the realisation that Hamlet and Phaedra may be dead, but that Theseus, Fortinbras and we ourselves have a duty to understand what has happened, and carry on with the business of living. This somewhat obscene uplift acknowledges the propriety of the dreadful events we have witnessed. They form a pattern, they have order and meaning. In an aesthetic, and, by extension, in a moral sense, they are acceptable. Tragedy has none of the horrible scream of negation with which Maldoror greets the vision of the eating God.

If tragedy fails to contain its subject matter the code breaks down. Hence the need for restricted focus. We witness just such a loss of control as we move from the planned universe of the seventeenth century to the scepticism of the eighteenth. There occurs a shift in the focus of concern. Tragedians of the eighteenth century write as if their heart is not in the business. Tragedy seems a storm in a tea-cup, a parish-pump affair. The artistic *avant-garde* is no longer disturbed by the fact that

statues may occasionally land on the heads of murderers. They
are worried by the possibility that the sky itself may fall in and
wipe out a whole community of innocents. With natural disasters such as the earthquake that destroyed Lisbon, with the
senseless devastation of a Seven Years War fought by enlight-
ened despots, contemporary thinkers begin to lose their sense of
the world as a place of order, regulated by the speedy succession
of effect upon cause. Instead they see chaos.

It is impossible to treat chaotic disaster in terms of tragedy.
There is no way in which such disaster can be motivated or
rendered meaningful. Without the benefit of such mitigation to
diminish the impact of the horror it portrays, tragedy cannot
be. So direct is the appeal of its language that a tragic treatment
unrelieved by the consolations of a tragic view of life would
over-stimulate our sense of fear and pity, and place us in a
state of numbed aesthetic shock; reaction becoming non-
reaction. It is just such a response that is all too often provoked
by famine-relief advertising. The iconographic impact is so
strong that one cannot afford to acknowledge it. Response is
atrophied and the reader quickly turns the page.

Large-scale disaster does not lend itself to tragedy. It can
deal with police actions, but cannot cope with the holocaust.
This is why it would be aesthetically disastrous to attempt a
tragedy about the death camps. The subject is so strong that
you must draw on other resources. In *The First Circle*
Solzhenitsyn does not take us to the core of Stalin's hell. As the
title implies, we remain on the outskirts, in the most agreeable
of prisons, a scientific research establishment. Although the
author makes his points effectively, he never overloads our 'will
to pity'. There is no Oxfam appeal here. It is the tone, and not
the subject-matter, that makes his book a very great novel. The
author achieves a mood of quiet gallows humour, a gentle ironic
detachment that permeates every sentence of the book, but
which is never brought to a crescendo. It is the ghostly presence
of black humour that makes pathos keep its distance. The
consequence of this restraint is that although the book reads
like a single high-pitched scream, that scream is articulate; it
can be heard through and through.

Another instance of black humour's ability to handle subjects
that would blow the fuses of a straightforward treatment is to be

found in an eyewitness account of the destruction of Dresden. In his novel *Slaughterhouse 5* Kurt Vonnegut Jnr writes how, just after the war, he thought he would find it easy to record his experience of the Dresden fire-storm. It proved virtually impossible and took him 25 years. *Slaughterhouse 5*, an extraordinarily lean book without an ounce of padding, finally achieves his purpose, but only by means of a strange, rarefied amalgam of whimsical science fiction, black humour and naked horror. He could not tell his story directly. In order to fit it into a work of art at all, he had to draw on the euphemising mediation of whimsy and the kind of jokes that do not make you laugh.

Black humour comes into its own when the scale of the disaster becomes too great to take seriously. It covers the area between tragedy and silence. Were *Candide* not rendered remote by the one-sidedness of its black humour, Voltaire's account of a meaningless and violent world would be unreadable.

Black humour does the same for the ludicrous disasters of the First World War—too great a monument to human stupidity to treat seriously; hence its clownesque rendering as a musical romp in *Oh! What a Lovely War!* Black humour takes up the running where tragedy comes to a halt, and it can take us to the very end; witness the climax of *Doctor Strangelove* in which a Texan airman sits astride the first H-bomb to drop, whooping down to oblivion. Black humour is the new language of the Apocalypse. Its capacity to handle terminal situations accounts for its important role in Jewish culture. When a race has lived under the threat of genocide for two thousand years, it needs a more powerful survival-strategy than a tragic sense of life. It needs that blend of courage, humour and utter resignation epitomised in Lenny Bruce's suicide bid, as he leaps out of a high window yelling 'Super Jew!'

In black humour Lautréamont found a language stronger than tragedy, a language that enabled him to describe a cruel arbitrary world, in which there could be no order, in the sense required by tragedy, because God, the ultimate source of all order, was himself the embodiment of chaos. Black humour enabled Lautréamont to describe the most unspeakable acts of violence, to paint a picture of the utmost blackness, and still be read.

The Ideology of the Absurd

Ducasse does not intend the world of Maldoror to be a direct representation of his own. It was at once an account of the dream-life of his world, and an extrapolation, a piece of research into the conceivable limits of chaos and iniquity, just as *Poésies* would investigate the opposite extreme of orthodoxy and order. But today's reader may feel that time has altered the significance of *Les Chants*, that they have shifted to centre-field; no longer a surrealist possibility, they have taken on the reality of a news bulletin. One can imagine Maldoror asking, 'Whatever happened to Sharon Tate?'

CHAPTER EIGHT

Anatomy of a Nightmare

Lautréamont was really born in 1920. Fifty years earlier Isidore Ducasse had written two books, but these only became generally known with surrealism. The surrealist poets such as Breton, Eluard and Aragon really created Lautréamont, and put him on their new map of European culture.

Surrealism represents the most radical rejection of official culture. It rejected the high priests of European consciousness, because that consciousness created the institutionalised barbarity of Verdun and the Somme. Moreover, traditional culture, founded on realism, common sense and profitability, was also responsible for the creation of the divided self. It had turned man into a schizoid creature through the exclusive attention it paid to his rational experience. The straight world, with its empirical tools for the analysis of our waking life, could measure, calculate and observe. It equipped man for work, gave him mastery over his physical environment. But the exclusive attention it paid to externals, to the world of machines and data-processing, atrophied his dream life.

It is true that commonsense culture acknowledged the world of inner space, but only to reject it, relegating it to the role of the entertainer, the *folle du logis*. Imagination was all very well after hours. In artists it was highly desirable, enabling them to produce good and interesting work, which, if recognised soon enough by the art-broker, might be had very cheap, and constitute an investment with a growth rate far exceeding that of any blue-chip equity. *The Times* regularly publishes an index that shows the performance of the various sectors of the art world, expressed in the idiom of a stock-market report.

The surrealists sought to re-authenticate our dream-life, to recognise that it was not subordinate to the waking world: the part it played in our existence was quite as important. Their ultimate aim, perhaps the most ambitious of any artistic movement, was to restore man to his original state of unified harmony. They sought to bring the broken halves of his being together and weld them into a new whole. They looked for a union of the scientific and the imaginative—a synthesis that would transcend all contradictions, a glorious fusion of love and work, reality and the dream.

For them the sub-conscious was much more than a source of agreeable images; it was a reality quite as valid as that of the waking world, which must be explored and charted. Only if we could understand it could we hope to achieve the marriage of waking and dreaming.

Consequently they were particularly interested in artists who displayed real imaginative authenticity, who captured the intensity and atmosphere of the dream world. They championed writers such as Poe, Maturin, Novalis and above all Lautréamont. Not just because their fantasies made the hair stand on end—whose hair could still stand on end in 1918?— but because the excitement their work generated proved that their testimonies were true. These were authors who had found a key that would unlock gates to an inner reality every bit as valid as the world of Balzac or Dickens.

The surrealists saw Lautréamont as the most powerful dreamer of them all. Every line he wrote rang with authenticity, spoke eloquently of the world of dream. He exerted a tremendous influence on them and their admiration for him was unqualified.

This is not to say that Lautréamont was a surrealist. He had no interest in the synthesis that they were searching for. He was more concerned with man's relationship to his culture-pattern, than with some occult quest for the union of opposites. To see him through the focus of surrealism is to get an intense but one-sided view. Because the surrealists distrusted consciousness, and by-passed its control with devices such as hypnosis and automatic writing, they assumed that Lautréamont, in order to achieve his extraordinary projection of dream and fantasy, must himself have been an automatic, instinctive creator. In my view he was perhaps the most deliberate and lucid writer imaginable. What the surrealists could only achieve by switching off the light, and plunging, pen in hand, into darkness, he spelt out by day.

Surrealist literature and painting can give the feeling of a strange and distorted world that is nevertheless uncannily familiar. The landscapes of Dali, Chirico and Max Ernst combine the conflicting characteristics of known and unknown. André Breton's poetry makes no sense, and yet it works, although we cannot say why. Surrealist art translates us into another world, but one which is nonetheless part of our own experience. We lack the language and the mental equipment to elucidate it, but we feel it to be authentic nonetheless. It is this quality of imaginative authenticity that Lautréamont shares with the surrealists.

He has an extraordinary command over the language of dream or, more specifically, the language of nightmare. Regardless of interpretation or cultural significance, anyone who is sympathetic to this kind of imaginative literature, whose mind is open to the truth that lies beneath the *frisson* he feels as he reads *The Monk, Arthur Gordon Pym* or *Moby Dick*, will find that Lautréamont takes him through to the other side; through the mirror that Cocteau's Orpheus had to pass through to find his Eurydice in the Kingdom of Death.

The following account of a child's nightmare paints a picture that is shifted slightly to one side of reality, without being so grotesque that its extravagance overwhelms us. As realistic as a surrealist landscape, it is every bit as disturbing :

It is midnight; from the Bastille to the Madeleine there is not a single omnibus in sight. I am mistaken; one turns up suddenly, as if from underground. The few remaining passersby look at it curiously for it does not seem like any other. Sitting on top are men with a fixed gaze, like dead fish. They are jammed up against each other, and appear lifeless; yet the regulation number of passengers has not been exceeded. When the driver whips his horses, it is as if the whip were moving the arm, and not the arm the whip. What can this strange collection of silent creatures be? Are they from the moon? There are times when you might think so; but they look more like corpses. The omnibus, in a hurry to reach the end of the line, eats up the ground, and makes the paving stones crack . . . On it goes. . . ! But a shapeless mass pursues it desperately in its tracks, in the dust. 'Stop, I beg you : stop . . . I've been walking all day and my feet are swollen . . . I've eaten nothing since yesterday . . . My parents have abandoned me ... I don't know what to do ... I'm going home and I'll soon get there if you take me ... I'm eight years old and I trust you.' On, on it goes! But a shapeless mass pursues it despairingly in its tracks in the dust. One of the cold-eyed men nudges his neighbour and appears to express displeasure at the silvery groans that reach his ear. The other nods imperceptibly in agreement and withdraws into the immobility of his egotism like a tortoise into its shell.[1]

As in the paintings of Magritte, the scene is profoundly disturbing. The gentlemen are not altogether real, they are a little too stiff, too dead. It does not feel quite right, but not quite right is quite enough to be profoundly disturbing.

Lautréamont's imagination is utterly at home in the landscape of nightmare. He never feels hampered by the rules that regulate waking reality. *Les Chants* describe a place in which animals and even stones have voices:

There are times in life when man, with his lice-ridden hair, stares wildly on the green membranes of space, for he seems to hear before him the whooping ironic mockery of a phantom. He staggers and bows his head : it is the voice of conscience that he hears. Then he flies out of his house, quick as a lunatic ... But the yellow phantom does not lose sight of him, and runs after him with equal speed. Sometimes, in a storm-tossed night, when legions of flying octopus, looking like crows in the distance, soar above the clouds, and fly swiftly to the cities of humanity, charged with the mission of warning them to change their way of life, the pebble's sombre eye beholds two beings pass in the lightning's flash, one behind the other: and wiping a furtive tear of compassion from its frozen eye it cries 'It is no more than he deserves ...' Having said so, it resumes its fierce attitude, and continues, trembling fitfully, to observe the manhunt and the great lips of the vagina of darkness, whence flow ceaselessly, like a river, gigantic shadowy spermatozoa, that take flight through the mournful ether, masking nature herself with the vast span of their bats' wings, and the solitary legions of octopus are saddened by the sight of these silent, nameless fulgurations.[2]

The tone of hysteria suggests that the narrator is overpowered by the intensity and madness of his vision. This world is the creation of a bedlam of the mind; it distorts or inverts the relationships and scales of the waking world. The very elements have their roles inverted, as octopus fly through the air, stones have eyes that weep and space is made of green membranes and is full of bat-winged spermatozoa. We may identify single words such as *bat* and *wing*, but we cannot recognise their combinations.

Lautréamont distorts and destroys the essential matrices through which we decode reality. His distortions threaten our sense of space, of what is 'up' and what is 'down', our ability to judge the relative size of images formed on the retina. A vision such as this leaves us totally lost, because Lautréamont cuts at the very components of the grid, eroding what J. G. Ballard referred to as 'the jigs and props of our consciousness'.

His distortions of scale can expand animals to grotesque proportions, creating creatures such as 'a glow-worm as tall as a house'.[3] Although the creature is utterly strange, it can still be conceived of and envisaged. The trouble with most monsters, for example the creations of H. P. Lovecraft, is that they must either remain shapeless, or else lose much of their power to terrify. In *At The Mountains Of Madness,* Lovecraft attempts the description of his 'Old Ones'; the result is disappointing. Quite simply they are too difficult to visualise, and lose much of their alien quality through description. Language can only describe the unknown in terms of the known, and in a horror story such description automatically defuses the bomb.

By relying on change of scale and inversion of the natural order, Lautréamont retains the precise visual quality, the crispness of focus that is an essential ingredient of dream, without sacrificing his sense of the grotesque. It is easier to visualise a forty-foot glow-worm or a giant beetle 'no bigger than a cow',[4] than a snark or a boojum. But such creatures are no less unnerving for being described in visual terms.

True to the principle that the dream world is an inversion of natural order, it is the giant insect and the proliferation of insect life that forms the centre of Lautréamont's nightmare. One of its principal protagonists is the louse:

There exists a creature that men nourish at their own expense. They owe it nothing; but they fear it. It does not like wine, but prefers blood, and if its legitimate needs were not satisfied it would be capable, by virtue of an occult power, of growing as big as an elephant, crushing men like young corn. See how it is respected accordingly, how it is accompanied by a dog-like veneration, how it is held in high esteem above the rest of creation. It is accorded our heads as a throne, and it fastens its claws on the root of our hair, with dignity. In time, when it is fat and getting on in years, in emulation of the practice of an ancient race, it is killed to spare it the pangs of old age. It is given a sumptuous funeral, like a hero, and the bier, which conducts it directly to the lid of the tomb, is borne, shoulder-high, by the principal citizens. Over the damp earth that the gravedigger stirs with his sagacious shovel are pronounced colourful orations about the immortality of the soul, about the insignificance of earthly life, about the mysterious ways of Providence, and marble closes, for ever, on this toil-filled existence, now a mere cadaver. The crowd thins out, and night soon covers the cemetery walls with its shadows.

But, mankind, be comforted in your sense of grief and loss. Behold its teeming family that approaches : he bequeathed it to you freely, that your despair be less intense, that it be relieved by the charming presence of these peevish little freaks, that will in time become resplendent lice, clothed in a remarkable beauty, monsters with a philosopher's gait. Its motherly wing has hatched several dozen eggs on your hair that has been withered by the relentless sucking of these redoubtable strangers. The time will soon come when the eggs hatch. Have no fear, they will soon grow up, adolescent philosophers, in this brief life. They will grow so big that they will make you feel it, with their claws and suckers.

You do not know why they do not devour the bones of your skull, and why they are content to pump out the quintessence of your blood. I will soon tell you : it is because they are not strong enough. Be sure that, if their jaws were cut to the scale of their infinite desires, the brain, the retina, the spinal column, your whole body would go. Like a drop of water . . . Woe betide the cachalot that fights a louse. It will be devoured in a trice, despite its size. Not even the tail would remain to tell its story. The elephant lets you caress it. The louse does not. I would not recommend you to try that dangerous experiment. Beware, if you have hair on your hand, or if it be made of blood and bones. You'll lose your fingers. They will crack as they would under torture. The skin disappears as if magicked away. Lice cannot do as much damage as their imagination can conceive. If you meet a louse, pass on by and do not lick the papillae of its tongue. You might have an accident. It's been known.[5]

The intense aggression that insect-life offers humanity strikes a deep chord in the imagination. It is easier to relate to warm-blooded animals than to insects, which differ from ourselves in almost every physical respect. So foreign are they that they represent a devastating threat, a rich source of nightmare; witness the traumatic role of the tarantula or scorpion under the bed in safari movies. The scale-change implicit in all Lautréamont's dreams of insect-life amplifies the threat enormously. Once the insect reaches the proportions that compel one to think of it in terms of a human module, the psychic intensity of the threat is unlimited. This is why insect forms offer science-fiction writers such a marvellous metaphor with which to describe alien invaders. In H. G. Wells' *War of the Worlds* the invaders look like giant insects: sufficiently familiar for us to be able to conceive of them, they are so utterly alien to our mammalian attitudes that their presence is extraordinarily disturbing.

Lautréamont uses distortions of the human face as another source of terror. The destruction of the face is an image that cuts at the archetypal bedrock on which we found our perceptual and cognitive attitudes. Figures such as the sphinx, with a human head and an animal's body, feel a great deal more human than figures such as the god Anubis, with its dog's head on a human frame. In terms of sheer volume, it is Anubis that possesses the greater proportion of humanity, but we certainly feel the sphinx to be the more human of the two. The human identity card begins from the neck up. This is why images attacking or distorting the face are so disturbing. Hence the impact of expressions such as 'my hyena's face',[6] and 'the Eternal One with his viper's countenance'.[7] Going beyond the most extreme disfigurement, they threaten our very being. Once the face goes, so too do humanity and the divine attributes; nothing remains but mindless animal aggression.

Despite its originality and psychic force, Lautréamont's

writing is never inaccessible. There are no communication breakdowns. He describes the utterly original landscape of his dream-life in terms that neither diminish its originality nor render it unrecognisable. He uses a public code to convey messages of the utmost privacy. His images appear the wildest of inventions, yet they are totally appropriate. Witness this description of God, lying dead-drunk in the middle of the road:

> He sprawled in the road, his clothes torn. His lower lip sagged like a soporific cable; his teeth were unwashed, and dust mingled with his wavy locks of gold. . . . Rivers of wine filled the ruts, dug by the jerky convulsions of his shoulders. Pig-faced brutishness covered him with its protecting wings, and looked lovingly on.[8]

One does not have to have seen a *câble somnifère* to get the feel of the expression, and the sense of monumental listless drooping. The image has a rightness that overrides the normal restrictions of sense and reality.

The poet is equally successful when covering a larger canvas, in set-pieces such as the traumatic vision of the eating God. One of the great purple passages of the French literary underground, it reveals Lautréamont's talent for the invention of episodes that come very close to myth.

If we understand by myth the account of a series of imaginary events that possesses a significance beyond entertainment value, events that embody in concrete form some quintessential truth that cannot be re-expressed in abstract terms without an impoverishment of meaning, then Lautréamont is a truly mythic writer. Visions such as the eating God translate us into a world of *significant* dream. A disciple of Jung's, Karl Kerenyi, writes of a tribe which had a dream-oriented culture. It divided dreams into 'big' and 'little'. Little dreams were private affairs of concern to the dreamer alone. Big dreams had a general relevance and their dreamer must relate them to the tribe.

Lautréamont is a dreamer of big dreams. The emblem of the eating God takes on a significance well beyond Maldoror's cry of terror. But this is not to say that it is allegorical. It cannot be reduced to the sum of its symbolic parts. It exists in its own right as a vision, leaving us free to draw our own conclusions. Lautréamont has bridged the gap, which has proved

fatal to more than one artist, between metaphysical reflection
and intense poetic imagery. Rather than tell his readers what to
think, he makes a powerful appeal to their visual sense, and
strikes an echo at the very base of our cultural memory. He
communicates personal images to us with such ease, because
his imagination seems to have special drawing rights on the
bank of universal archetypes. Time and again it generates very
personal images that maintain the kind of universal psychic
intensity that one associates with archetypal situations.

The eating God is such an archetype. In the description of
God's throne of shit and gold, we find one of Freud's archetypal
associations—muck and money are synonyms in the world of
dream. Lautréamont creates a vision directly reminiscent of
Goya's terrifying picture of Saturn gnawing at his offspring.
But at no stage do we feel that he is writing his vision after
Goya, that it constitutes an iconographic reference. It is
Maldoror's vision. Through imaginative coincidence—the same
force that encouraged Jung to evolve his theory of archetypes
and the universal unconscious—Lautréamont's imagination
echoes that of his predecessors.

One can only speculate as to why Lautréamont should have
created such archetypal images. But if we look at the image of
the eating God and its ancestors in Greek mythology, we can
see that aspects of the elemental myths have something in
common with the enterprise of Lautréamont.

Both the myths and *Les Chants* seek to clarify the ways of
God to man. Primitive Greek literature, moreover, reflects the
traumatic experience of the imposition of culture on nature,
taboo on anarchy, law on society. The principal concern of its
tragedies is the consequences of the infringement of prescriptions
that have a force exceeding that of mere law. To break them is
to put yourself beyond the pale of human society, to be banished
from the state of culture. These are not laws but taboos, based on
kinship. *Hippolytus* and *Oedipus Rex* are concerned with
incest, *Electra* with matricide, *Agamemnon* with parricide. The
plays investigate taboos which form the basic constituents of
human society. Incest taboo is the only institution that has been
claimed to be universal to all forms of society. Its status as a
social universal is a disputed point among anthropologists, but it

is at least the only institution that is a serious candidate for that title.

The aesthetic and mythopoeic imagination may well have taken the incest taboo as representative of the very principle of social man. We shall be seeing that infringement of this taboo plays a vital role in *Les Chants*. The myths on which Greek tragedy is founded thus seem concerned with the impact of the principle of taboo upon the psyche. Lautréamont investigates a very similar area of human experience. The eating God is a myth about the birth of law and order. It calls the principle of authority into question, suggesting that God the father, or the schoolmaster Hinstin, *in loco parentis*, might not be the benevolent creature that his traditions would have him be.

The reason why Lautréamont generates such mythic situations, why his writing is so rich in archetypal material, may be found in the imaginative posture that he adopts. Since he is thinking about fundamentals, his imagination tends to express itself through fundamental motifs. They coincide with the traditional material of myth because his viewpoint is so close to the one on which those myths were founded. He thinks in such basic terms that it is scarcely surprising that he should sometimes echo myths that form the bedrock of our cultural heritage.

CHAPTER NINE

The Language of Dream

Lautréamont's archetypal affiliations make it clear that no one's imagination is free. We have here one of the most orginal poets in Western literature, who makes a radical break with the patterns of his culture in every respect save his imagination. His imagery fits, with uncanny smoothness, into a table of the characteristic imaginative types of European culture. He may liberate himself in every other respect, but Lautréamont cannot free the one aspect of his being that he assumes to be unique.

Imagination is formed by culture as much as any language is. We can understand Lautréamont because he uses a code, the French language, that we share with him. He also imagines in a language, and it is in so far as we share that language also that his poetry reaches us as an emotive communication.

The most striking quality of the language of his dream-life is its dynamic aggression. A vast proportion of the book describes Maldoror's attacks on God and humanity. The following passage reveals the transitive quality of his imagination. Lautréamont is describing his conception of his hero.

> Indeed, I tear away the mask from his [man's] treacherous muddy face, and one by one . . . I cast down the sublime lies with which he has deceived himself . . . This is why my hero has attracted irreconcilable hate by attacking man, who believed himself to be invulnerable, by undermining his absurd philanthropic tirades; they have piled up in his books like grains of sand . . . It is not enough to carve the statue of goodness on the frontispiece of library parchment. Man! You stand there, naked as a worm, before my sword of diamond![1]

The passage forms a nodal point that brings a number of themes together. Maldoror's powerful aggressive movement, rendered by the violent transitive verbs, has an educational function. Aggression and education become associated.

Maldoror the triumphant aggressor dominates his weak and cowering pupil. Man is described as a worm, he is the passive victim of the educational onslaught. The most important image of the passage is the diamond sword of judgment. It combines essential strains of his imagery. In diamond we have purity, light and extreme hardness, associated with the sharp cutting edge of the sword, which of course also has phallic connotations. All these are in turn linked with the idea of the sword as the instrument of judgment before which man quails.

Lautréamont usually founds his rhetoric of aggression on cutting, tearing, sharp edges. Maldoror never employs a blunt instrument. The knife is his favourite weapon. Indeed the sharp blade cutting into something soft is perhaps the dominant image of the entire work. It is a metaphor that is encountered in a variety of contexts. We find it used casually: 'A cruel war threatened to drive its harpoon into the breast of two enemy countries.'[2] It is in no respect the unique preserve of Maldoror. In the following example a similar action is used to describe man's riposte: 'Man, that sublime monkey, has already pierced my chest with his lance of porphyry.'[3] The language of sharpness and cutting is also, curiously, used to describe the precise analytic quality of mental events: 'You drive your sneering scalpel into my consciousness.'[4] On another occasion he refers to pursuing truth with the 'scalpel of analysis'. He uses similar language to describe mathematics—a discipline for which the author had a boundless admiration. It is a weapon with which he will fight both man and God—presumably because it is a pure discipline, free from the contamination of humanism and cultural bias. The imaginative equation of purity, cutting and lucidity bring us back to the diamond sword. Mathematics will enable him to 'plunge into man's viscera a sharp dagger that will for ever remain in his body'.[5]

Images of purity of substance account for some extraordinary descriptions of Maldoror's person. His tongue is a 'triple barb of platinum'.[6] His features contrast with the soft and yielding characteristics of man's 'muddy face'. Maldoror has a 'face of platinum',[7] he is 'the man with lips of bronze',[8] 'of sulphur',[9] 'of jasper',[10] 'the man with jasper pupils',[11] 'with sapphire lips'.[12] Maldoror is practically a diamond sword himself.

Maldoror has no monopoly over epithets of hardness. God is

dressed in a 'cruel sapphire tunic'.[13] There is sometimes a strange
confusion between Maldoror and God: both are aggressors, and
both express themselves through hardness and cutting.

In opposition to these images of purity and attack, the
human body is always available for indignity, punishment and
mutilation. It is savaged and sodomised without relief, as if the
imagination were treating it with aggressive and puritanical
asceticism. Maldoror, in contrast, hardly has a body. The
poetry scarcely dwells on his physical substance except to
describe his face as hard and pure. He is not subject to physical
restrictions, but slips in and out of his body at will. To attack
the dragon of hope he becomes an eagle, to attack God an
octopus. He shares with the divine and angelic protagonists of
the book a talent for instant metamorphosis. Metamorphosis is
a sign of superior rank in the hierarchy; bodily restriction a sign
of inferiority.

Maldoror also associates triumph with dreams of flight and
transcendence: 'If the earth were covered with lice ... What a
sight! I would contemplate it from the air, motionless on
angel's wings.'[14]

But despite this emphasis on purity, flight and aggression,
these are not the hero's only postures. All these motifs stand as
the positive elements in a series of plus/minus oppositions.
Lautréamont's imagination experiences flight as the positive
counterpart to falling, just as the imagination opposes air to the
contrasting element of water. This is why archetypal images of
falling take the form of a fall into water—Icarus. Water
acquires a negative tonality, and is often used to render mortality or passing time, in opposition to dreams of transcendence
and immortality that express themselves in the image of soaring
flight.

One of the crucial passages of *Les Chants* is a lyrical address
to the ocean. In Godard's *Weekend* a guerrilla fighter in the
NLF Seine-et-Oise recites a long invocation, accompanied by a
drummer. It is Lautréamont's 'Je te salue, vieil océan . . .' The
violence and radicalism of *Les Chants* are utterly appropriate
to *Weekend*'s apocalyptic conclusion.

Lautréamont uses water imagery to suggest the dark, doom-
ridden and anti-rational cradle of monsters, as opposed to the
angelic world of the air. It also represents the natural world

from which man is absent. Maldoror's sole non-aggressive sexual act, conducted on a basis of mutual consent, takes place in the sea with a giant female shark. Along with their praise of lucidity and consciousness, *Les Chants* acknowledge the sea as a place of hidden depths and secrecy, containing the shark, the most aggressive creature in the poet's bestiary.

Aggressive movement is not the only condition in which we find Maldoror. He also appears as a passive victim, in a state of total paralysis. The passive–active polarity plays a crucial part in the homosexual eroticism of *Les Chants*. To love is to be the executioner, to be made love to the tortured victim. Sex is seen through the focus of violence. The author writes of the joys of '[hurting] a creature and [being loved] by the same creature : the greatest happiness one can conceive of.'[15] Elsewhere we find Maldoror in a passive role in the following phrase: 'I shall adorn my body with scented garlands, for that holocaust of expiation.'[16] And again we find the masochistic imperative: 'Shut me up for life in a dark prison, with scorpions to keep me company in my captivity, or tear out one of my eyes so that it falls to the ground.'[17]

The counterpart to the dream of aggression emerges more fully on two occasions. Twice Maldoror features in a major episode in a state of paralysis. The theme of paralysis is hinted at early in the book in passages that describe Maldoror attempting to speak, only to find his throat tightening and stifling the effort. Frustration of immense effort is an essential ingredient of paralysis dreams. Paralysis lacks imaginative impact unless it is set against an overwhelming desire to move. This emerges in an episode that sets paralysis against a dream of pure aggression. The author dreams he becomes a pig free to kill and wound to his fill. The dream culminates in his apotheosis, alone in his resplendent grandeur. His return to human form is accompanied by paralysis:

My feet were paralysed; no movement threatened the truth of this enforced immobility. It was in the midst of supernatural efforts to continue on my way that I awoke, and felt myself turning back into a man.[18]

These allusions to paralysis prepare for the two great night-

91

mares of enforced immobility. In the first, we are told that a 'man or a stone or a tree' is speaking :

I am dirty. Lice gnaw me. Pigs are sick when they look at me. The scabs and scars of leprosy have scaled my skin, covered with yellowing pus. I do not know the water of rivers, the dew of clouds. On my nape, as on a dung-heap, there grows an enormous mushroom ... Seated on a shapeless piece of furniture I have not stirred my limbs for four centuries. My feet have taken root and, up to my belly, they form a kind of living vegetation full of base parasites, not yet a plant but no longer flesh. Yet still my heart beats. But how should it beat did not the putrefaction and the emanations of my carcass (I dare not call it a body) nourish it copiously? A family of toads has taken up residence under my left arm-pit, and when one of them moves it tickles me. Take care that one doesn't escape and come to scratch the inside of your ear with its mouth; it might enter your brain next. Beneath my right arm-pit there is a chameleon that hunts them ceaselessly in order not to die of hunger: we all have to live. But, when one side completely outwits the other, they can think of nothing better to do than casually to suck the delicate fat that covers my ribs: I'm used to it. An evil viper has eaten my cock and taken its place : the villain made me a eunuch. Oh ! If I had been able to defend myself with my paralysed arms; but I rather think that they have turned into bundles of wood. Whatever may have become of them, it must be pointed out that blood no longer suffuses them with its redness. Two little hedgehogs, that have stopped growing, have tossed my testicles to a dog, who did not refuse them: they washed the skin out carefully, and settled inside. My anus has been intercepted by a crab; encouraged by my passivity, he guards the entrance with his claws, and causes me much pain. Two jelly-fish came from across the seas, drawn by an expectation that was not disappointed. They looked carefully at the two fleshy parts that form the human posterior, and, fixing themselves to their convex curve, they have crushed them so totally by a constant pressure, that the two pieces of flesh have vanished, leaving two monsters, come from the viscous realm, alike in

their colour, form and ferocity. Speak not of my spine, it is a
sword.[19]

The passage is the exact counterpart of Maldoror's regular
aspiration to purity, mobility and liberation from the body. He
is plunged into a viscous, paralysed world in which the slowest
monster can outstrip him. He is an utterly passive victim, his
phallic attributes, his diamond sword, quite literally eaten away.
He is at the bottom of the imaginative axis that stretches from
monster to angel, from Caliban to Ariel. Maldoror is the
prisoner of his body, and the passage is saturated with corporeal
imagery.

The second great scene of paralysis is less intense, but more
specific. It concludes the fifth canto and is one of the two
alternative endings with which Lautréamont closes Les Chants.
The final episode features a victorious Maldoror: the total
aggressor, he triumphs over God and executes his definitive act
of violence. The penultimate canto portrays him as the
paralysed and consenting victim of a divine vengeance:

> Each night, at the time when sleep has reached the peak of
> its intensity, an old spider of thte giant kind slowly lifts its
> head through a hole in the floor, in a corner of the room. It
> listens carefully in case any buzzing sound still vibrates its
> mandibulae in the atmosphere. In view of the fact that it
> is an insect, it could do no less, if it wishes to enrich the
> treasure-house of literature with brilliant personifications,
> than attribute mandibulae to the buzzing. Once assured that
> silence reigns, it withdraws, one after another, from the
> depths of its nest, and without the help of meditation, the
> various parts of its body, and advances deliberately towards
> my bed. Strange to relate, though I can stave off sleep and
> nightmare, I feel totally paralysed, as it climbs up the ebony
> supports of my satin couch. Its legs seize my throat, it sucks
> my blood with its belly. Just that! How many litres of a
> crimson liquor, the name of which you know well, has it not
> drunk.[20]

Maldoror vaguely recollects having empowered it to do so. On
this, the final occasion that it drinks, it reminds him of the
circumstances of the pact :

The spider had opened its belly, out of which flew two adolescents robed in blue, with flaming swords in their hands, who took their place on either side of the bed, as if henceforth to guard the sanctuary of sleep.[21]

They are two of Maldoror's lover-victims. An archangel ordered them to turn themselves into a giant spider in order to punish Maldoror for the space of ten years, a term now accomplished. He himself had realised that 'it is better to submit oneself to this irrevocable decree'.[22] Maldoror awakens to see two forms fly heavenward, arms linked. He stares at the moonlight in a state of dry-mouthed horror, waiting 'for morning's change of scene to bring a derisory relief to my shattered heart'.[23] We leave him suffering at dawn, or longing for dawn: *le mal d'aurore*.

Les Chants thus has a dual conclusion: two endings rendering the extremes of paralysis and aggression. We can begin to understand a little more about the ending and gain an insight into the meaning of the dominant image patterns by matching these against some of the patterns of imagery that the imagination of Western man tends to generate.

Typologies of the imagination show that there is a degree of consistency to be found in imagery in general. Poets who share the same image-patterns tend to share the same values. But to suggest that poets have image-patterns in common is not, of course, to say that they make the same statements: the fact that they write in the same language does not mean that they all say the same thing.

A general study of the nature and significance of certain image-patterns has been convincingly carried out by a French scholar with anthropological leanings. George Durand's *Les structures anthropologiques de l'imaginaire* has proved helpful in the analysis of the imagery of other poets, notably of Baudelaire. It also throws light on Lautréamont.

Durand concludes his work with a table showing the various kinds of imagination that he describes. The principal characteristics of the imagery of *Les Chants* correspond almost exactly to one of his categories, which he describes as the *régime diurne* —the realm of day.

Briefly its key concepts, words and images are as follows. It has an ideological content that is idealising, polemically assertive and so divisive as to be schizoid. It uses antithetical argument. It values symmetry, precision, sharp geometric forms. It tends to isolate, exclude, separate, and operates along an axis of contradiction and identity—rather than use strategies of compromise. Its dominant physical reflex is a striving to be upright—as opposed to seeking the foetal position. Its key verbs oppose separating to mixing, flying to falling. Its adjectives pair off into antithetical couples: pure/soiled, light/dark, high/low. Its dominant symbol is the sword or sceptre. Its nouns also pair off: light/darkness, summit/abyss, pure air/foul air, heaven/hell, heroic weapon/bond—the example given is Alexander and the Gordian knot—baptism/pollution, hero/monster, angel/ animal, wing/reptile. Key images are the sun, blue sky, the eye of the father, armour, circumcision, tonsure, high places, birds and Jupiter.

This account of Durand's table has scarcely been adapted to suit Lautréamont, and yet it contains all his dominant characteristics. Images of sharpness and cutting, the diamond sword, are particularly relevant. Images of violent aggression also fit: movement is opposed to paralysis, cutting to binding. Images of flight are equally important. Maldoror flies, and leaves his body behind him. The *régime* also matches *Les Chants* in its valuation of purity of essence and extremist attitudes. The two opposing and mutually contradictory works, *Les Chants* and *Poésies,* are the very incarnation of antithesis.

The *régime* puts a premium on judgment, which it represents with the all-seeing eye of the father. In *Les Chants* it is Maldoror who takes over the father's role.

Associated with images of flight is the important part played by birds in *Les Chants*. Not only does Maldoror change into an eagle, and is also described as a condor, but birds are also used as an image that renders the design of the entire work.

Les Chants contains its fair share of images of verticality. For example the poet associates the upright with the phallus, when he describes the fate of a giant hair which God left behind after a visit to a brothel. It is desperately crying to beat its way out of the whore's crib. Initially vertical, it is weakened by its efforts to escape and rejoin its owner, and gradually loses its verticality. The connotations of divine *dégonflage* require no comment.

The real interest of Lautréamont's relationship to the *régime* lies in the information that Durand supplies about its significance. The world of the *régime* is violently antithetical, a world of conflict and opposition. Its images are asserted *against* their opposites. Images are in themselves tacit acknowledgments of the existence of their counterparts; flight, verticality, purity, spirituality, aggression and transcendence imply their antitheses, falling, the earth, time, water, shadow, darkness, the limitations of the flesh, paralysis, animality and the restrictions of an earthbound existence.

Seen in the light of these patterns Lautréamont's poetry clearly has as its basic dynamic an upward striving towards liberation from the confines of human culture: man's muddy face. Moreover the poet has painted both sides of the picture. The sea is set against images of purity and spirituality. It is the abode of monsters. The role of paralysis and containment also becomes clear: the antithesis against which Maldoror's eventual triumph will be set. Reference to the pattern can therefore illuminate both sides of his imagery. His imagination gives, it is true, much more prominence to the positive elements, but it also acknowledges the negative counterparts.

The ambitions and aspirations of the *régime* also have their relevance to *Les Chants*. They seek to overcome the limitations of man's mortal condition, and aspire to a transcendence that is a form of divinity. Victor Hugo, one of the great exponents of the *régime diurne,* notably in his later years—mystic, visionary, social tribune—is a perfect case in point.

This aspiration to transcendence is usually expressed in dreams of flight—the Shelley syndrome—a longing to float over the earth, and perhaps eventually to be joined with God in Abraham's bosom. Maldoror provides a fascinating variant of this longing. He seeks not to be re-united with God, but, like Nietzsche, to replace him. Hence the occasional confusions between God and Maldoror. Genuinely God's rival, he aspires to take his place. On one occasion, we find him gnawing on the skull of his conscience, in a remarkable echo of the eating God himself. In his ambition to rape the universe he manifests a will to power that matches even Nietzsche in its intensity. The dream of man becoming God is as important to Maldoror as it is to Zarathustra or Ivan Karamazov. But where Nietzsche proclaims God's death, and Karamazov declines to acknowledge his existence, seeing in that denial a mandate to parricide. Maldoror founds his ambitions on a conflation of parricide and deicide. He experiences the death of God as a murder, and genuinely aspires to replace him. Maldoror, for example, inverts the image of the eye of the father-judge from which the wicked cannot hide. It is Maldoror whose all-seeing eye keeps God under surveillance : 'I shall always remain on guard, keeping my eye on Him.'[24] Similarly we find God playing Maldoror's part as homosexual aggressor. He flays an adolescent alive when he visits the brothel, and on another occasion, the author concludes an invocation to *pédérastes incompréhensibles* : 'It was a winter's night. As the wind whistled through the pine-trees the Creator opened his door in the midst of darkness and let in a pederast.'[25]

The supplanting of God by Maldoror is not the only respect in which Lautréamont deviates from the standard pattern of the *régime*. The typical imagination experiences the antithetical pattern as a straining away from the negative pole, toward the ethereal plane of the positive. This is not the case with Lautréamont. He accords the sea, usually given a hostile treatment as a place of disaster, all the veneration that he gives to flight—although the sea is an image of disaster nonetheless. Evil, usually opposed to good, is unremittingly celebrated. But the author does not simply treat evil as if it were good. Good gets an equally powerful celebration in *Poésies*. The handling of good and evil illustrate his unique approach to writing. The author does not express personal attitudes and preferences; he unfolds the circumstances in which such attitudes and preferences are formed. He takes no sides, does not oppose thesis to antithesis, negative to positive. He simply describes the two extremes as carefully as possible. This explains the extraordinary relationship of *Les Chants* to *Poésies*; they represent the limits of antithesis. The author is no more committed to one than to the other, he simply describes both—the absolute moral opposites that form the right- and left-hand limits of our culture. Unlike any other writer of his time, the author is not writing about himself and his longings, but about the basis on which ideas of the self are founded. Hence he gives the two extremes equal loading, not only in the relation between his two works, but in *Les Chants* themselves, in which so-called negative images such as the sea are given unprejudiced treatment.

97

It is this dispassionate admission of the negative dimension that explains the work's double conclusion. His impartiality is such that he declines to take sides. The two contrasting endings, one negative, one positive, echo, in miniature, the structure of his literary life's work. They represent the treatment afforded, on a larger scale, to thesis and antithesis by *Les Chants* and *Poésies*.

This is not to say that the author was in any way familiar with the complex pattern of Durand's archetypology. It was simply the case that when it came to evaluating the various possibilities of his imagination, he remained uncommitted. Declining to use the terminology of positive and negative, he made no value-judgments. His imagery unfolds in terms of contrast, not conflict. Where Hugo, who generates identical image patterns, chooses to arrange these on a vertical axis, creating a chain of being that stretches from the prison-planet Saturn to the pure spirituality of the astral plane, Lautréamont turns that axis through ninety degrees. He creates a horizontal chain, its extremities representing the limits of human experience within a certain cultural and imaginative pattern.

CHAPTER TEN

The Pattern of *Les Chants*

Nineteenth-century fiction is based on a convention which assumes that the novel reflects a reality beyond the work itself. The novel tells a story 'about' something. Not only does this principle apply to novels of contemporary life, it also applies to the fantasies of a Novalis or a Jules Verne. Even in cases such as these the convention makes believe, and presupposes, the existence of a hypothetical non-linguistic reality.

Almost any work of any length written in this era is of a linear nature. This quality is the direct consequence of its role as a reflector of non-linguistic reality. It is admirably illustrated by the epigraph to *Le Rouge et le Noir*: 'The novel is a mirror that moves along a road.' Such novels are so constructed that pieces may continually be tacked onto their end. This linear progression is most perfectly embodied in the *Bildungsromane*, the whole series of sentimental educations that play so large a part in the European fiction of the first half of the century. They usually take the form of quests, in which each new episode contributes to the formation of the hero's consciousness. They are situated more or less firmly on a time scale—as opposed to the space scale embodied in the journey-motif of eighteenth-century novels. So strong has been the influence of this form that we have come to think of books in which the hero develops on a time scale as *the* form of the novel. Proust is a crowning example.

Much of this century's *avant-garde* fiction has been written against this conception of the novel form. Although *Ulysses*, by its title, makes a somewhat ironic acknowledgment of the journey motif, *Finnegan's Wake* explodes the sense of temporal continuity once and for all. Modern writers reject the convention that requires the novel to reflect an exterior reality; a set of characters and events that are deemed to pre-exist the book itself. Instead they write in such a way that the novel can be seen to generate its own reality—to spin its world out of itself.

French 'new novelists' such as Robbe-Grillet and Philippe Sollers seek to escape from the tyranny of the linear model. In *Dans Le Labyrinthe* Robbe-Grillet begins with a description of a room. Outside it there is a soldier standing under a street-lamp. The author returns to the description of the room itself, devoting great attention to the contents of a picture hanging on the wall. It represents a café scene, that suddenly comes to life. A door in the café opens, and the same soldier walks in. The novel blends one plane of reality into the next, until the only reality the reader can trust is the reality of the printed word.

Sollers also writes novels that do not purport to refer to anything beyond the world of the book itself. One of his works, *Nombres*, is based on an algebraic formula, and it is this that dictates the contents of the book.

This was by no means the first generation to experiment with non-linear forms. Gide made great use of them as early as *Les Caves du Vatican*, but by far the most prestigious and eccentric author of non-linear works was Raymond Roussel.

Roussel was a dilettante mathematician and the author of some of the strangest works of fiction written in this century. He constructed his work on utterly non-linear principles. There is no question of their reflecting, or creating, reality. His works are quite simply word-games. They use a combination of crossword-puzzle techniques, algebraic equations and puns. His aesthetic is based on the idea of a physical object, a text, that is made to undergo certain programmed transformations.

Roussel takes a set of phonemes—the representation of the sounds of language—that have a certain meaning. He then alters one of the phonemes, thereby altering the meaning completely. He then invents a fiction which describes the transformation of the first set of phonemes into the second:

> I would choose two words, virtually identical, then I would add similar words taken in two different senses, thereby producing a sort of equation of facts.[1]

He takes a phrase;

Les lettres du blanc sur les bandes du vieux billard.

This becomes:

Les lettres du blanc sur les bandes du vieux pillard.

In the first phrase *lettres* means the typographic sign, *blanc* means chalk, *bandes* wrappers, *billard* a billiard-table.

In the second the words mean missives, a white man, hordes and pirate respectively.

The two meanings make up the two terms of an equation. The story consists of the account of a series of extraordinary events that translate us from the left-hand meaning to the right-hand one. The transformation takes place for arbitrary textual and linguistic reasons, that have nothing to do with non-linguistic reality or with linear narrative.

Considerable proportions of *Les Chants* and *Poésies* are constructed on non-linear principles. The notion of non-linearity can be clarified by reference to two expressions from the vocabulary of linguistics. They are used to describe the two sets of possible relations that may obtain between linguistic elements such as words. The first relationship, known as 'syntagmatic', may, for the sake of this argument, be thought of as a linear relationship. If we take the word *cat*, there is a series of words that could be appropriately placed immediately before it, another that might succeed it. In the first category one would find words such as *the, a, ginger*, in the second *ate, purred, which*. Such words are said to form syntagmatic relationships with the word *cat*. But words may also be related to it in another way. *Cat* might be thought of as heading a class of words such as *dog, horse, cow*. Alternatively it might head a differently constituted class, that would number *bat, mat, sat*, or *cot* and *cut* among its members. Such a class is constructed on analogical as opposed to linear principles. The relationship between its members is known as 'paradigmatic'.

Poésies is constructed almost entirely on paradigmatic principles. In that considerable proportions of it consist of the re-writing of Pascal and Vauvenargues, these passages stand in a paradigmatic relationship to the originals; they are analogous to them. Had they picked up where the originals concluded, the relationship would have been syntagmatic.

Thus Ducasse writes: 'Generosity enjoys the happiness of others, as if it were responsible for it.'[2] This is based on a maxim of Vauvenargues: 'Generosity suffers from the misfortune of others, as if it were responsible for it.'

Where linear writing is essentially purposive, with a sense of direction, paradigmatic writing is static and circular. It repeats the same movement over and over again, apparently re-covering the same ground, but rendering the movement richer and fuller with every pass. It makes the reader think about the transformations that it brings about. We think about the way the text changes, and, more important, about the radical shifts in meaning that those changes produce; even though they are themselves the product of chance or some random principle—the decision to turn all negatives into positives, as Lautréamont did with Vauvenargues. Not only do such transformations create new meanings, they create new contexts in which meaning may occur; they show how meaning may be the product of an encounter between the deliberate expressive intention of a writer—Vauvenargues—and blind chance. Once again Lautréamont invites us to consider the bizarre interplay between form and meaning. He places us at the cross-roads of language itself.

He hints at his interest in shifts of meaning that can be achieved by transformational techniques when he invites us to: 'Try . . . to transport into your imagination the various modifications of my cadaverous reason.'³ Modification is indeed the word. This non-linear approach to writing has fascinating implications for the art of this century. *Implication* is a most appropriate expression in this context, for its etymology—fold-in—recalls the term used by William Burroughs to describe his own technique.

Much of Burroughs' work consists of apparently random incorporation of arbitrary fragments of materials into a patchwork assembly. Its only unity may well be the unity of the printed page. He plays with the effects of random juxtaposition. But his writing is only superficially reminiscent of the totally arbitrary re-assemblies of surrealist cut-ups. It retains an underlying unity, since the fragments are all projections of the author's fantasy life, and ultimately have a common ground. The final effect is of a non-linear, homogeneous and yet delicately shifting pattern; nodes of meaning that form and dissolve before us. The reader comes to understand that meaning does not exist beyond the printed word, it is an integral part of the word itself and of its particular situation.

Ducasse's transformations of Vauvenargues have a similar effect. The knowledge that Vauvenargues is being transformed into Ducasse plays an important part in our experience. Similarly large portions of *Les Chants* themselves consist of transformations of other works, for example an encyclopedia of natural history, that acquire a very different meaning in their new context:

> I was still a long way off; for, like the skuas, restless birds that always seem hungry, and who prefer the seas surrounding the poles, and only advance into temperate zones by accident, I was not at peace.[4]

The shift in significance achieved by the folding-in of such pieces points to the important role played by context in the process of comprehension. What seems a totally appropriate passage in a piece of natural history becomes a surrealistic image in its new situation. The context creates in us certain expectations, in the light of which we filter the fresh input of information.

Sergei Eisenstein demonstrated the extraordinary importance of contextual feed-back—the way that what has happened controls our expectations of what is going to happen—by taking a shot of an actor in close-up. His expression was neutral. He cut this shot into a number of sequences. Each one ended with a cut to the actor's face, and each had its own feeling tone, ranging from extreme sorrow to extreme elation. The sequences were shown to an audience. They were asked to gauge the quality of the actor's expression as a reaction shot, in each instance, and to grade their results. They proceeded to do so, finding him more or less effective as the case might be. So powerful was the contextual feed-back that it occurred to no one that the expression was identical in every instance. Lautréamont makes his own uses of contextual feed-back with his fold-ins and transformations.

He operates another series of transformations of a different order. It will be recalled that the first version of the first canto was published separately. Between the first and the final publication it undergoes substantial paradigmatic modifications.

These transform the text from an autobiography into something madder and less personal. The transformations alter the tone of the whole canto, but only one detail is changed. A certain passage originally read as follows:

> Ah! Dazet, you whose soul is inseparable from my own; you, the fairest son of woman, though an adolescent still; you whose name resembles that of the greatest friend of Byron's youth; you in whom reign . . .

What sounded like a piece of sentimental homosexual rhetoric becomes:

> Oh octopus of the silken gaze! you, whose soul is inseparable from my own; you, the fairest of the inhabitants of the terrestrial globe, commanding a seraglio of four hundred suckers; you in whom reign . . .[5]

On another occasion a reference to Dazet is transformed into a *rhinolophe*—a kind of bat with a horse-shoe crest on its nose. Dazet also becomes: 'oh venerable louse, you whose body is without wing-sheaths'.[6] Again we move from a sentimental climate into the strangest of bestiaries. The culminating example of this practice is stranger still. What began as:

> As for you, young man, despair not: for you have a friend in the vampire, despite your belief to the contrary. And counting Dazet you have two friends . . .

in the final version becomes:

> . . . and counting the itch-mite that gives you mange, you have two friends![7]

Lautréamont's transformational assault on his sources raises the question of the whole pattern of taboo that our culture has wrapped around the business of writing. The inviolability of signature is the greatest taboo of all. We have come to regard the final draft of a sonnet or play as an act of absolute expression. Nothing about the work, not even a comma, may be altered, without bringing the whole fabric of our culture crashing about us. Authorship must remain inviolate. The copyright laws are merely the legal echo of the aura of sanctity that surrounds the artistic signature; that signature without which no work of art is complete.

One might ask when a Vermeer is not a Vermeer? The answer of course is when it is a van Meegeren. But in what sense is a genuine forgery less real than the real thing? Does a work of art lie that incorporates, *as part of the painting*, a series of marks that look like Picasso's signature?

Any exploration of this question of originality, that is not governed by a need for authenticity bound up with the values of the market-place, cannot but help demonstrate the absurdity of the problem. But it is not the absurdity so much as the narrowness of this view that is regrettable. Without this taboo the scope for amusing, nonsensical and deeply serious trans-formations would be unlimited. The iconoclasm of *dada* sketched out a few of the possibilities, such as the moustache that Duchamp drew on the face of the Mona Lisa. But that moustache only scratched the surface.

CHAPTER ELEVEN

The Build to Climax

The use of transformational techniques is not restricted to minor aspects of the book. The entire work forms a paradigmatic series, each stage of which represents a more fully developed version of an initial situation. The final version treats in elaborate and explicit detail a motif that was initially no more than hinted at.

In this way the structure of *Les Chants* resembles the form of a detective story. With the exception of a very few writers of the *avant-garde*—Borges being the outstanding example—the detective story is the only fictional form, certainly the only popular form, to rely on paradigmatic development.

The standard novel of detection opens its paradigm with a crime, of which we are told some but not all of the circumstances. In the company of the detective we move through a series of events ideally intended to increase our knowledge of the circumstances of the crime. The events can be thought of as devices that amplify those circumstances—amplify in the electronic sense, a process that increases the power and modulation of a signal. The climax comes when those involved all assemble in the library and the detective goes through the circumstances of the crime for the last time. His reconstruction is now complete, the murderer revealed and the paradigm concluded.

It would be over-ambitious to suggest that Lautréamont's use of paradigmatic development acknowledges his debt to the detective story. Although he echoes the surface structure of the form in the final canto, it is a far cry from that to the gradual elaboration of the series of images that are fully realised in the final episodes of *Les Chants*. However the *raison d'être* of the technique raises important and intriguing questions, that are nonetheless important and intriguing for being quite unanswerable.

The transformations may be thought of in two quite different ways. One theory would suggest that they are the work of a calculating craftsman: a Borgesian lover of theorems and chess problems, who plans each move meticulously.

The alternative view would be that Lautréamont is not working out the transformations; rather that the transformations are working themselves out in him. Such a view suggests that we have grossly overestimated the role of calculation, at the expense of intense imaginative extravagance; the traumatic workings of a tortured soul. The transformations would be the result of an unconscious process. A series of images gradually impose themselves with an ever-increasing insistence and precision, until they are fully verbalised, faced up to in the light of consciousness.

This 'coming to consciousness' constitutes the resolution of some complex trauma, and the poetry takes on a psychoanalytic role, which features its author as both patient and analyst. The work would become what a Jungian analyst would call a 'process of individuation'. The outcome of a successful process of auto-therapy of this kind would probably bring about the dispersal of the patient's creative urge. The artist is motivated by his complex, which can only express itself through the oblique language of his art. Once the subject has faced up to the complex he no longer needs that language, and the drive to create disappears.

Such cases have been known, or supposed, to have happened. The plot structures and oppositions of Racine's theatre, and his eventual silence, have been most convincingly explained in these terms. Such an explanation of the dissolution of the creative drive would certainly account for the aridity of *Poésies*. Their tone is utterly prosaic, and lacks the imaginative extravagance of *Les Chants*. They could well be the work of a writer who has attained creative sterility, his drive exhausted by the acts of exorcism that terminate *Les Chants*. The author has laid his ghosts and the work of his imagination is done.

The pattern of transformation begins with the muted allusion to an event that will eventually find full elaboration. Thus, in the early stages of the book, Maldoror's cruelty is restrained and diluted by Gothick rhetoric. His first murder is by long distance. He makes a youth die in his sleep, and the murder takes the shape of a dream sequence. Maldoror's transformation from potential to actual murderer is not a development, it is the gradual re-rendering of a single image, treated with an increasing richness of orchestration and intensity.

Another example of this movement begins with a phrase

that reads: 'The angel of sleep [was] himself struck a mortal blow on the brow by an unknown stone.'[1] The motif of a missile striking a semi-divine creature recurs when Maldoror, in a church, throws a stone that severs a magic silver lamp from its hangings. It is an angel in disguise. This image is subsequently transformed into the angelic crab that Maldoror fells in the final canto. The image attains its final form or apotheosis when Maldoror shoots down God himself. It is transformed from a trivial allusion into a major incident of the conclusion.

The most interesting transformations are those that build up to the events concluding the fifth and sixth cantos. Taken in isolation the two scenes of Maldoror paralysed and Maldoror the ultimate aggressor appear unmotivated fantasies. In fact they are the culmination of a series of episodes; scenes that pull together many different threads, they come to seem highly motivated and hence very acceptable.

This may be illustrated by the strangest of all the episodes of *Les Chants*. In the middle of the sixth canto Maldoror comes upon a madman, who, uninvited, tells his story. Known as the episode of the Three Marguerites, it has an extraordinary surrealistic incongruity:

'My father was a carpenter in the Rue de la Verrerie ... May the death of the three Marguerites rest on his conscience and the canary's beak forever peck at the axis of his eyeball. He was in the habit of getting drunk; at such times, when he came home after having been from grog-shop to grog-shop, his fury almost boundless, he lashed out at each and every thing that caught his eye. After a while, as a result of the admonitions of his friends, he reformed completely and became uncommunicative. No one, not even my mother, dared to go near him. He nourished a secret grudge against the idea of duty that prevented him from doing as he pleased. I had bought a canary for my three sisters; it was for my three sisters that I had bought a canary. They placed it in a cage, over the door, and passers-by would stop to listen to it, to admire its elusive grace and study its wise ways. On more than one occasion my father ordered the cage to be removed, for he believed that the canary was mocking him, tossing him a garland of vocalist's trills. He went to unhook the cage and, blind with anger, slipped off the chair. A small scratch on the knee was his reward. After devoting a few instants to pressing a shaving on the swollen part, he lowered the leg of his trousers, frowned, proceeded with greater care, tucked the cage under his arm and went to the back of his workshop. There, despite the cries and entreaties of his family (we were all attached to that bird, that seemed to us to be the spirit of the house), he crushed the osier cage with his studded heels, while a plane, whirling around his head, kept the spectators at bay. Chance would have it that the canary did not die at once; this feathery snow-flake was still alive despite the bloodstains. The carpenter went off, slamming the door behind him. My mother and I tried to stop life from leaving the bird; it was dying, and the movement of its wings appeared a mere reflection of its death throes.

In the meantime the three Marguerites, seeing that all hope was lost, took each other's hand, in common accord, and the living chain went and squatted under the stairs, beside our bitch's kennel, having pushed back a barrel of fat. My mother persisted in her task, holding the canary in her fingers, seeking to revive it with her breath. As for me, I ran despairingly through the house, banging against furniture and tools. Now and again one of my sisters showed her head from beneath the stairs to find out how the poor bird was doing, and withdrew it sadly. The bitch had left her kennel, and, as if understanding the extent of our loss, she licked the three Marguerites' dresses with the sterile tongue of consolation. The canary only had a few moments to live. One of my sisters (the youngest) took her turn and advanced her head into the semi-darkness caused by the decrease in light. She saw my mother grow pale, and the bird, which had raised its head for an instant, the final manifestation of its nervous system, fell back between her fingers, forever dead. She told her sisters the news. They uttered no quivering sound of complaint, not a murmur. Silence reigned in the workshop. You could only hear the intermittent cracking of pieces of cage that, as a result of the wood's elasticity, were partially going back to their original positions. The three Marguerites shed not a tear, and their faces did not lose their ruddy freshness; they remained still. They dragged themselves inside the kennel, and stretched out on the straw, side by side; while the bitch, the passive witness of their action, looked on in amazement. Several times my mother called them; they uttered no sound of acknowledgment. Tired by the recent emotions, they were probably asleep . . . She followed the bitch, who pulled at her dress, towards the kennel. She bent down and poked her head inside. The sight that she was in a position to see, over and above the unhealthy exaggerations of a mother's fear, must have been distressing, as I see it. I lit a candle and offered it to her; in that way not a detail escaped her. She withdrew her head, covered with pieces of straw, from the premature tomb, and said to me, 'The three Marguerites are dead.' As we could not get them out, for, remember this, they were wrapped tightly in each others' arms, I went and fetched a hammer from the workshop, in order to break up the dog's dwelling. I set to immediately, and passers-by, those with imagination anyway, must have thought that we were not short of work. My mother, distressed by these delays, which were inevitable however, broke her nails on the planks. Finally the negative rescue operation was done; the kennel, split asunder, open on every side; and we removed the carpenter's daughters from its ruins, one after another, parting them with difficulty. My mother left the country. I have not seen my father since. As for me, they say I'm mad, and I beg for my living. I only know that the canary sings no more.[2]

Although the episode appears utterly arbitrary and quite lacking in contextual preparation, elements of the scene have been encountered before. This is the third occasion on which a group of girl-victims has been mentioned, silent, docile and weighed down with grief. Earlier Maldoror had placed upon the guillotine 'the tender grace of the necks of three young girls . . . who smiled at me sweetly'.[23] When God visits the brothel, once a convent, the nuns come out of their tombs in silent horror. This is another embryonic version of the same image: 'Here they come, dressed in their white shrouds. They do not speak; they hold hands.'[4]

The three Marguerites themselves form part of a larger and more important paradigm. They were described as a 'living chain', an expression that occurs in a number of passages, and forms one of the book's key paradigms. In this version the author associates the image with the eventual death of Mervyn, and with the design of the book itself:

> ... the stormy overflowing of a love which has resolved not to appease its thirst with the human race. A famished love that would devour itself were it not to seek its nourishment in celestial fictions : finally creating a pyramid of seraphim ... he will weave them into an ellipse which he will turn about him, and ... [you] will see ... a human being carried off to the cellar of hell by a garland of living camellias![5]

The passage contains a number of important nodal points. The garland of living camellias is a version of the garland of the three Marguerites—a garland by virtue of a Roussel-like play on their name which also means *daisy*. In this passage the living garland represents the seraphim who will form a garland by joining arms, as did the two boy victims who flew heavenward, hand in hand, on leaving the spider's belly. The creation of celestial fictions, i.e. Lautréamont's literary creation, is seen as a mode of transcendence. Maldoror circles the living garland about his head. This motion is anticipated in the carpenter's gesture with his plane. It also plays an important part in the final and most complete version of the paradigm. The final scene of the book describes Maldoror twirling Mervyn about his head. As he lets go, his victim grabs for a garland of daisies—*immortelles*. In their company he completes his course, and is draped across the dome of the Panthéon, in which the immortals of France lie buried.

The cross-references that this word-play sets up provide an excellent illustration of how transformation works. The poet is concerned with purely verbal relationships; he follows the paradigm of word-shape, not meaning-shape. He moves freely from immortal seraphim to *immortelles* (flowers).

Through this paradigm we can see the emergence of the dominant theme of the book. Characteristic of the *régime diurne*, it is a quest for transcendence which will be achieved through the chain of seraphim. Maldoror/Lautréamont's love is such that humanity cannot satisfy it. It must invent ideal, celestial fictions. These are in fact the pile of adolescent corpses on which Maldoror, figuratively, climbs to the top of the

111

column. The feeling tone of this passage—a dream of purity arrived at through homosexual murder—is remarkably close to the tone of Genet. He too finds beauty and purity in the extremes of homosexual violence and criminality. For him, as for Lautréamont, the adolescent victim, essentially uncontaminated by base characteristics, is a figure of purity through whose death one may achieve transcendence.

The penultimate conclusion, in which Maldoror is vampirised and himself a victim, is also prepared for. Early in the book he is threatened by vampiric nightmares that make him bleed from his nose and ears. Elsewhere he is terrified by a shadow on the wall. That shadow will, in due course, be transformed into the spider. It is typical of the transformation process that the paradigm increases in clarity and substance. What begins as a mere shadow, the hypothesis of nightmare, gradually evolves into a reality.

Similarly the punitive adolescents who sit at his bedside are first met on an unreal plane, as fictions:

> Let us recall the names of those imaginary beings, of angelic nature, which my pen . . . has drawn from a brain . . . they shine with a light that radiates from their own being.[6]

This anticipates their final apparition. Not only do Réginald and Elsseneur, as they are known, also shine with their own light, there is a strange linguistic parallel between their being 'drawn from a brain' and drawn from a spider's belly. What was initially a metaphor is again brought to life as a statement of fact.

The young men's blood-sucking role is also anticipated. In an invocation to the *rhinolophe* and originally to Dazet we read:

> Some say that you approached me in order to suck the remaining blood from my body: why is this hypothesis not a reality![7]

There is another reference to the sucking of blood in the man–stone–tree sequence:

> It cannot be that a scorpion has established its abode and its sharp claws in the centre of my lacerated eye-socket; I think it is a pair of vigorous pincers that is crushing my optic nerves. Yet, I agree, that the blood filling the bowl has been taken from my veins by an invisible torturer while I slept last night.[8]

The paradigm is here developed from a hypothesis to the work of an invisible agent, and reaches its climax in the spider sequence in which Maldoror can see what is happening. No longer a nightmare fantasy, these creatures are neither hypothetical nor invisible. The point is made by a significant contradiction in terms: 'We are no longer in a narrative ... Alas! we are now in real life.'[9] According to the psycho-analytic thesis the transition from dreaming to waking brings the moment when Ducasse is almost able to confront his trauma without the mediation of fiction. What was at first only bearable as a dream of an imaginary character, can now be expressed as part of that character's waking life. This hypothesis is confirmed by the fact that Réginald and Elsseneur tell Maldoror at length of his cruelty towards them: it seems he had forgotten. Made to face up to his sado-eroticism, he no longer requires the defensive strategies provided by the unreal fragmentation of dream.

We now come to the most important transformation of all, Maldoror's execution of Mervyn:

His hands tied behind his back, he walks straight ahead, as if going to the scaffold, and yet he is guilty of no offence. They arrive in the circular confines of the Place Vendôme. From the top of the massive column, a man, leaning against the square balustrade, over fifty metres above the ground, has thrown down a cable which falls to the ground a few paces away from Aghone [the brother of the three Marguerites]. Once you know how, you can get things done quickly, but I must say that he didn't take long to tie Mervyn's feet to the end of the cord. The rhinoceros had discovered what was to happen. Bathed in sweat, he appeared panting at the corner of the Rue Castiglione. He didn't even have the satisfaction of joining battle. The individual, who was keeping an eye on things from the top of the column, loaded his revolver, took careful aim and pulled the trigger. The Commodore [Mervyn's father], who had taken to begging in the streets from the day that what he supposed to be his son's madness had begun, and his mother, known as Snow White because of her extreme pallor, advanced their breasts in order to protect the rhinoceros. In vain. The bullet holed its hide like a gimlet; you might have thought, with logic apparently on your side, that death must inevitably ensue. But we know that the substance of the Lord had entered into that pachyderm. He withdrew sadly . . . [Maldoror] retrieves the cord and its weighty attachment with a sharp jerk of his wrist. The oscillations of the rope . . . swing Mervyn, who is upside down, to and fro. His hands grasp a long garland of evergreens that joins two consecutive corners of the base, against which his head bangs. He carries off with him, into the air, that which was not a fixed point. Having piled up a great proportion of the cable, in the form of ellipses, one on top of the other, in such a way that Mervyn dangles half-way down the bronze obelisk, the escaped convict swings to the adolescent, with his right hand, in a uniform rotating motion of increasing speed, moving on a plane parallel to the column's axis; his left hand lets out the snake-like rolls of cable at his feet. The sling whistles through the air; Mervyn's body follows, centrifugal force always keeping it away from the centre, preserving its moving position equidistant, in an aerial circumference independent of matter. The civilised savage lets go little by little, until he reaches the other end, which he holds on to with a firm fist, like a steel bar. He starts to run round the balustrade, holding on to the rail with one hand. This changes the plane in which the cable moves, and increases the tension which was already considerable. Henceforth, it turns majestically in a horizontal plane, having passed through several oblique planes in succession. The right angle formed by the column and the vegetable rope has equal sides. The renegade's arm and the murdering rope blend into linear unity, like the tiny particles in a ray of light penetrating a dark room. The theorems of mechanics enable me to talk like this; alas! it is well known that one force added to another produces a result consisting of the two original forces! Who would dare to suggest that the line of rope would not already have broken, were it not for the strength of the athlete, the quality of the hemp? The golden-haired corsair, suddenly and at the same time, both stops and releases the cable. The reaction to this movement, that is so unlike the preceding ones, makes the joints of the balustrade crack. Mervyn, followed by the cord, resembles a comet trailing its floating tail behind it. The iron ring of the slip-knot, glittering in the sunlight, seeks to render the illusion complete. As he describes his parabola, the condemned youth cleaves the atmosphere, reaches and crosses the left bank ... and his corpse strikes the dome of the Panthéon, whilst the rope embraces part of the upper face of the cupola in its coils. It is upon this spherical convex surface, resembling an orange in form alone, that at any hour of the day or night you may see a dried skeleton hanging.[10]

The manner of Mervyn's death is so bizarre and elaborate that the author must have had an obsessive need to make him die as he did. The need may be partly explained by the role played by the episode as the culmination of a large number of paradigms.

One of the most important is the paradigm of circular movement—the *tourbillon* (whirlwind, vortex, swirl). We find references to the *tourbillon* the tide makes around a rock. This becomes Mervyn's movement around the rock of the column. There are references to a demon whirling in the gust of a storm. The movement from demon to Maldoror is not difficult. Birds also play an important part in the paradigm. We find them flying in circles: 'like two condors of the Andes, they love to soar in concentric circles, ... nourishing themselves on the purest essence of light.'[11] More specifically, wasps 'flutter around columns like thick waves of black hair'.[12]

The circular movement is itself frequently anticipated. In the light of the final episode expressions such as the following become comprehensible: 'I shall direct against you the sling of a terrible accusation.'[13]

There are a series of expressions that associate the final episode and its earlier versions with the themes of the *régime diurne*. The pattern has been seen to include birds and, in the last example, judgment. More important still is the fact that the movement is executed by a pure adolescent. An essential attribute of the poet's erotic vision of the adolescent is his long hair. Maldoror's victims all have flowing locks that stream behind them and sometimes get torn off. This is another affiliation with the *régime diurne,* one of whose characteristic motifs was the theme of tonsure.

Bachelard identified the image of long hair being shorn with the theme of schoolboy revolt. He suggests that Ducasse might have had to endure an enforced hair-cut at school, and that the experience is reflected in his work as a scalp and, *a fortiori*, a castration complex. Certainly it makes an excellent image for enforced conformity to the culture-pattern, suggesting a possible treatment of *Les Chants* as a sado-masochistic tribal rock musical–*Hair* produced by the Marquis de Sade.

Lautréamont is hair-obsessed. He builds an entire scene on the hair God left behind in the brothel. He also describes the luckless man whose mother and wife strung him up by the hair, because he refused to sleep with his mother. He struggles 'with movements that merely serve to separate the roots of my hair from my head'.[14] A more direct anticipation of the final episode occurs when Maldoror seizes an adolescent by the hair,

> with an arm of iron, and made him turn through the air with such speed, that the hair was left in my hand and the body, impelled by centrifugal force, crashed against the trunk of an oak. I know full well that one day his hair was left in my hand ... I accomplished this infamous act, as his body was driven by centrifugal force.[15]

Mervyn's body in flight is described with its hair streaming behind it. The image is anticipated by a number of references to comets, that will eventually be transformed into Mervyn:

> When a comet, at night, appears suddenly in a part of the sky ... it displays to the inhabitants of earth and to crickets its shining vaporous tail.[16]

On another occasion Maldoror himself becomes a comet:

> You see me cross bloody space, a new phenomenon, like a terrifying comet.[17]

Mervyn's final contact with the dome of the Panthéon is also anticipated, as a strange philosophical metaphor:

> The apparition of this flaming comet will no longer shine, like a sad subject of fanatical curiosity, on the façade of your disappointed observation.[18]

Maldoror's final spinning action is prepared by incidents such as the following:

> It is he who forces me to make him turn like a top, with the steel-lashed whip.[19]

116

and:

> the muscular arm of a woman of the people seizes her by the hair as the whirlwind seizes the leaf.[20]

The following passage is more explicit still:

> I could, lifting your virgin body with an arm of iron, take you by the feet, whirl you round me, like a sling, concentrate my strength when describing the final circuit, and throw you against the wall.[21]

What is the significance of the coming together of all these paradigms in the final episode? Not only does it conclude the book, it also sums it up. A passive adolescent victim of irreproachable purity is destroyed by a savagely active sadistic maniac. The relationship is a clear projection of the work's antithetical structure. The theme of transcendence is expressed in images of purity, flight and the garland. The rude and ironic interruption of flight by the Panthéon provides the negative counterweight. It is an intensification of the Icarus myth, the archetypal myth of transcendence followed by a fall. Mervyn does not just fall out of the sky; he is hurled out of it. Where Icarus moves on a vertical axis, Mervyn flies on a horizontal one.

In his introduction to the final canto the author prepares us for his definitive statement, with the following carefully phrased expression:

> Would you suggest that because, as if in play, I have insulted man, the Creator, and myself, in my explicable hyperboles, my mission is complete? No; the most important part of my work is yet to be done. Henceforth, the puppet-strings of the novel will move the three characters mentioned above: a less abstract force will thereby be imparted to them.[22]

The passage brings the book's metaphors to life: what was once a hyperbole, a figure of speech, will become a real hyperbole—the figure executed by Mervyn in space. The force will certainly be less abstract; it will be the centrifugal force that drives him through the air. Transformation again takes us from fantasy to reality—a point driven home in the concluding lines. They tell us that if we do not believe the author, we should go to the Panthéon and see for ourselves.

Both the crucial transformations, Maldoror paralysed,

117

Maldoror triumphant, contain this movement from dream to reality. What began in a world of Gothick imagery, extravagant rhetoric and erotic fantasies of violence, ends as a nightmare that takes place in broad daylight in the Place Vendôme. The world of *Les Chants* is deceptively simple. We tend to assume that what begins as fantasy must end as fantasy. Instead we move gradually from fantasy to nightmare in the streets.

Perhaps Ducasse began his work on a fantastic note in order to be able to say what he wished to say and still be read. After all fantasy, like black humour, is a distancing device. His true intention is to force our attention on the sick and violent myths by which his society lived. His work opens in the never-never land of a pseudo-romantic dream world. But the imagery is gradually transformed, preserving its violence but shifting its context until, suddenly, the aggressive fantasies are being played out in the streets of Paris. Had he begun as he ended the work would have been rejected as ludicrous. Instead he introduces us to violence by establishing a context—the world of *The Monk* and *Frankenstein*—in which violence is appropriate. Gradually he brings his readers to the point where they realise that they are reading about violence in quite a different context, and *still loving it*.

It may appear that they only find it so acceptable because they have been tricked into doing so, but the move from fantasy to reality does not end with *Les Chants*. History takes up the running. Hardly a year was to pass before the Communards pulled down the column in the Place Vendôme, and the forces of law and order would subsequently celebrate the Commune's fall with a blood-bath in which even Maldoror might have drowned. Lautréamont's mythology has come home to roost. As we think about violence in the streets, the mob violence of the Revolution, the massacres of the June Days, the repression of the Commune, or even the tear-gas and baton charges that played such an important part in the university education of the class of '68, we realise that we accept the conclusion of the sixth canto not because we have been tricked into doing so but because it is true. Admittedly we can no longer see Mervyn's skeleton hanging from the dome of the Panthéon, but then the events described in *Les Chants* took place a century ago, in the *ville lumière*—a city that keeps its monuments clean.

PART THREE

The Prison

CHAPTER TWELVE

A Room with a Limited View

Ducasse is obsessed with the knowledge that we are all held by the limits of our culture-pattern. However much we may resent it, we can only see what culture permits us to see, for it is culture that has created our grid, the particular set of categories through which we decode and classify reality. Throughout *Les Chants* the poet has sought to make us realise that there is nothing real about these categories, nothing in natural, as opposed to cultural reality, that makes it necessary for us to use those categories in the particular way that we do.

This is easily illustrated. The colour spectrum is an un-interrupted continuum. It is the cultural grid that divides it into colour categories. The categorisation of primary colours varies from language to language; even within the European language group. Thus Russian has two primary colours that, broadly speaking, may be said to cover the range of colours we embrace in the single category of blue. Non-European languages display an even greater margin of divergence. Hanunóo, a language of the Philippines, has four main colour terms that are based on lightness, wetness, darkness and dryness. The language classifies colours in a manner quite foreign to our culture. For example it will apply to a shiny wet *brown* section of bamboo a term that is also applied to *light green*.

Jorge Luis Borges provides a more fanciful illustration of the fact that linguistic categories are not based on universals. These, according to Borges, are the classes into which the Chinese used to divide animals: a. The Emperor's property; b. Em-balmed; c. Tame; d. Sucking-pigs; e. Sirens; f. Fabulous; g. Dogs off the leash; h. Included in this list; i. That rush around like mad things; j. Countless; k. Drawn with a fine camel-hair brush; l. Etc.; m. That have just broken a jug; n. That look like flies in the distance.

We are consequently all restricted by the vision of reality imposed upon us by our categories. We can only see what

Lautréamont terms partial truth, and 'what an abundant source of errors and mistakes is all partial truth!'[1] Our culture-pattern is formed for us by factors almost entirely beyond our control. It creates for us a yoke made of 'the habits formed by age, books, the contact of our fellows and our inherent character'.[2]

The author suggests that much of what we think of as ourselves, the unique and inalienable part of us, is the product of chance and of circumstances external to the self. Lautréamont's drive towards apotheosis is the outcome of the simple desire to be himself. It is a quest for purity in the chemical, as much as in the moral, sense; a quest that can only be dreamt of, but which can never be successfully completed. We will always remain 'imprisoned within the limits of our understanding'.[3]

No one can preserve themselves from culture's contamination. Inevitably, and, more important, imperceptibly, other peoples' values will infiltrate us all. Alas for revolutionaries and prophets of the cultural millennium, we are always doomed to be victims of partial truth. We are, to say the least, being ridden in blinkers; the only question for Ducasse is just who is the rider, and does he have kind hands?

Escape from partial truth is not possible because our system functions in terms of partial truth only. Our very existence is regulated in terms of a one-dimensional system so all-enveloping that those that live by it lack the mental equipment to judge it; so mesmerised are they by their particular state of culture that they cannot conceive of an alternative.

The greatest one-dimensional factor of all is language, and a brief study of the way in which we handle linguistic input is relevant, not only because it will show us precisely why language does constitute a one-dimensional situation, but for the much more important reason that the way we handle it is, I suspect, the way in which we process input of any kind.

The process of handling linguistic input is based on our unconscious capacity to break down the speech sounds we hear into two categories: those aspects of the sounds that function as linguistic signs, known as *signal*, and the rest, known as *noise*. Now we are programmed in such a way that we only take in signal, and to all intents and purposes do not hear noise at all. Our decoding system rejects and disregards anything that it classifies as noise. It is, for example, because of our particular classification of noise and signal that we do not notice, on the whole, that the *t* in *put* and the *t* in *tap* are in fact two different sounds. Because both sounds happen to make the same signal, we disregard the fact that they make a different *noise*. Differences in noise are rejected as irrelevant. They may exist but they do not really matter. It is because the difference between *l* and *r* is not relevant to their signalling system that the Chinese have great difficulty in distinguishing between the two sounds. It is equally hard for us to hear the difference between the four tones of Mandarin or the six tones of Vietnamese.

Any examination of the way in which language operates isolates, as being of paramount importance, this capacity to hive signal off from noise. We notice only what is linguistically relevant, and disregard the rest. It is probably in this way that we handle input of every description. We only absorb those aspects of the messages being sent to us that are classified as signal. In other words, we know only what we need to know.

But the whole basis of Lautréamont's thesis is *how do we know what we need to know*? Just who determines the signal–noise mix on our behalf? How do we know that the world is not full of rich and exciting things, infinitely more exciting than the six tones of Vietnamese, which will for ever pass unnoticed, because it has been decided for us that they are not important; that we don't need to know them; that they are noise?

It is scarcely surprising that the very root of language is so contaminated, since language is the medium through which culture reaches us. There is no escape from its influence short of an escape into autistic aphasia. As a mode of escape this is not far removed from Lautréamont's own wish to be 'alone in the intimacy of my reasoning'.[4] It is appropriate that language should be the weapon that culture employs to subjugate its victims, maintaining them in a condition of mesmerised acquiescence, for language is perhaps one of the two cultural universals. It is not a natural attribute. The so-called organs of speech— tongue, teeth, lips, larynx, palates, vocal cords, lungs, nasal cavity, etc.—all serve other purposes in the first instance, and have been adapted to the sending of signals.

Language, the essential creation of culture, controls and shapes our attitudes, telling us what we need to know and that only. When we speak or write, we may believe that we are expressing ourselves. But since the categories we employ are not of our choosing, what we say is not of our choice.

Lautréamont sees us as victims of a malevolent censorship that has created a particular signal/noise ratio from which there is no escape. A whole series of factors, from parental metaphysical toilet-training to the genial chidings of liberal, pipe-smoking and right-thinking university teachers, forces us into a pattern of collaboration and partial truth. When eventually arraigned for crimes against humanity, we will all be entitled to the defence that we were only obeying orders. Lautréamont does not see this purblind one-dimensional situation as the mere consequence of an unthinking paternalism that tries to cast its offspring in its own mould because it is too lazy to cope with the possibility that they might be different. The unthinking authoritarianism with which culture brings us to heel is founded on something more sinister than mere happenstance. We are in a position of partial truth because we live under censorship. But there is no censorship without a censor. In Lautréamont's world there is a censor; he is malevolent; his name is God.

Maldoror attacks God for keeping the lion's share of the truth to Himself. He has so conditioned our attitudes that we must needs see things His way. He is responsible for the creation of our grid. However Maldoror will mount an assault on Him, and try to get at the whole truth :

> I take it on myself to extract the remaining portions of intelligence which you did not want to give to man, because you knew you would be jealous were you to make him your equal, and which you brazenly concealed in your guts, cunning bandit, as if you didn't know that one day or another I would find them with my ever-open eye.[5]

Maldoror will take up the consumption of the forbidden fruit where Adam left off. He is not satisfied by the suggestion that partial ignorance is bliss. He will fight to secure the rest of the truth and his weapons will be cold reason, logic and mathematics. With these he will carve his way to the heart of the matter. Mathematics in particular he describes as a poisoned weapon with which 'I made the Creator himself descend from his pedestal, erected by the cowardice of man'.[6] This points to our own responsibility for our situation. We are guilty of collaboration by consensus. Man is stupid and cowardly enough to condone his own exploitation, to settle for half a loaf. Political analogies are appropriate here. The author presents the human race as an exploited but non-militant class, that has not yet reached the stage of the 'unhappy consciousness'. Maldoror, with his combination of unspeakable acts of violence and aspiration to divinity, goads man into seeing the truth about divinity itself, and, *a fortiori*, about all authoritarian situations from government to school. Maldoror seeks to bring about a *prise de conscience*, to make man realise which end of the stick he is holding, realise that the hand with which he grasps it does not smell of violets. In short he tries to create a revolutionary situation. This is why he is sceptical about the power of prayer in a world in which we are all prey to the eating God:

> How long will you maintain the mouldering cult of this unfeeling god, who is deaf to your prayers ... Look, he's not grateful, the hideous manitou.[7]

Maldoror sees God as the fountainhead of all authoritarianism. He has a vested interest in our virtue, but no inducement to be virtuous himself. This notion of divinity is incarnate in society in the principle of authority. It is the acceptance of this principle, of one's role as governed as opposed to governor, that is *the* constituent of civilisation as seen by *Les Chants*. Lautréamont suggests that the world-picture that we receive has not been made for us, but for those who derive pleasure from controlling us. We find whole areas of knowledge denied to us, classified as noise, because it would not be in the national interest for us to have access to them. The United States will shortly witness the creation of a central data-bank containing information on every citizen. It has been decided that it would not be in the national interest for citizens to have access to their own dossiers. We accept such situations on trust, because we feel that the authorities have our interests at heart. How do we know? Because they say so.

Culture is equated with submission to a malevolent and self-interested authority. Anything we may be told to the contrary is pure public-relations. Resistance is possible, but first you must want to resist. Only by thinking clearly, from first principles, will you think in a way that is not contaminated by the way they want you to think.

God encourages man to do good and avoid evil, in order to have a quiet life Himself: 'How should man consent to obey these severe laws, if the legislator himself is the first to refuse to be ruled by them?'[8] If he is to maintain law and order, God must have his actions concealed. After his apocalyptic trip to the brothel, in the course of which He spent the night with a whore, and flayed an adolescent alive, He tells the hair He left behind Him to cover up for Him:

> I am the Great All; yet, in one respect, I remain inferior to men . . . Tell them a daring lie, and say that I never left heaven, being perpetually preoccupied with the concerns of government.[9]

But His alibis are seldom water-tight. He allows Himself to be found drunk, sprawling in the middle of the road. He is also immensely cruel. His punishments do not fit the crime. Look, says Maldoror, at what He did to Satan, and he considers the Satan myth without using Man's frame of reference. Satan is condemned to eternal damnation 'for a trivial revolt which had no serious consequences'.[10] Cruelty goes well beyond this savage and punitive reprisal. There are times when God seems strangely like another kind old gentleman with a white beard, Uncle Sam himself: 'I have seen the creator spurring on his purposeless cruelty, starting fires in which old men and children perished.'[11] But of course in wars of national liberation there is no such thing as a civilian, so there can be no such thing as civilian bombing. This napalm comes to you by courtesy of Catch-22.

Moreover if we have the talent for self-destruction, the skill to manufacture petroleum jelly, guess who is responsible?

> It is thus that the Creator, keeping cool in the midst of the most appalling suffering, is able to extract, from their own being, seeds harmful to the inhabitants of this earth.[12]

The secret life of authority is cruel, obscenely violent, and given to debauchery and venal sex. But authority makes us see things its own way; it places us in a room with a limited view, a view that shows us nothing but sweetness and light.

126

CHAPTER THIRTEEN

Strategies of Escape

Lautréamont knows total escape to be impossible, but he does recommend ways of achieving at least a partial liberation. In order to free oneself from the restricted truth of culture, that culture must be broken down, element by element. Lautréamont's ambition is to be true to nature, not to the role that culture dictates he should adopt.

The pursuit of truth to nature dictates the course of the crucial final image pattern. The figure that Mervyn and Maldoror execute together represents totality, the sum of thesis and antithesis; they combine the fundamentally opposing motifs of the circle and the straight line. Mervyn describes a circle, then a straight line; Maldoror stands on the upright of the column, in the middle of the circular space of the Place Vendôme.

Before we feel that we are being required to read too much meaning into surrealistic fantasies, we should attend to a passage early in the first canto, in which the author warns the reader to take him seriously:

Pay no heed to the strange way in which I sing each one of these verses. Rest assured that the fundamental accents of poetry still maintain their essential claim upon my intelligence.[1]

It is with nature that the poet specifically associates his strange design. Nature for the poet seems to be the place where you may achieve totality, as opposed to culture, which requires us to see everything in terms of partial truth and choice.

Language, the mainstay of culture, is founded on choice. Virtually the first law of linguistics, as formulated by de Saussure, is that 'meaning implies choice'. This is to say that linguistic signs have no meaning in themselves. They derive their meaning from their place in a structured system, from their context. A sign is meaningful in so far as it may be seen to be different from any other sign that might occur in the same

127

position. 'In language there are only differences,' said de Saussure.

We recognise a linguistic sign, for example a speech sound, simply because it sounds different from any other speech sound that might have occurred in its place. 'Not x but y' is the vastly over-simplified account of the recognition process. Now 'y-ness', that is to say the qualities of the sign in question, may be defined by purely negative characteristics, its qualities of 'not-x-ness'. This is to say that language identifies units negatively; not by detecting what they are, but by perceiving them as distinct from what they are not. As users of language we are always obliged to choose; to eliminate some elements if we are to accept others.

This is equally true of cultural phenomena. The anthropologist Claude Lévi-Strauss achieved a major breakthrough in the study of primitive institutions with his recognition that certain areas of human behaviour, that appear beyond the conscious control of the individual and follow complex self-generating rules, function in the same way as language. Investigating kinship systems and myth he has largely succeeded in showing that seemingly haphazard and unrelated pieces of human behaviour may in fact form part of an organically structured system. Lévi-Strauss achieved his insights by considering the pieces of behaviour in terms of their symbolic roles as elements in what virtually amounted to a signalling system. He realised that their meaning was not to be derived from their intrinsic character, but from their situation in a wider pattern of like and unlike, a situation opposing them to other elements of a similar order. Once he could understand their role within their particular system, he was able to define their significance in the social organisation as a whole.

This thought of Lévi-Strauss has fascinating implications for the study of human institutions. He invites us to consider these as if they were structured systems that operate in a way that is basically the way of language itself. Just as the sounds *l* and *r* have significance in a particular system, because they are nodal points in the grid of that particular system, whereas in another system they might be totally meaningless, so it is with social institutions, and, ultimately, with entire cultures.

Each culture is obliged to select its nodal points from an

infinity of ungraded spectra—covering everything from possible speech-sounds to possible degrees of kinship. It is on the basis of its selections that it creates its particular grid. All cultures are, in the final analysis, founded on choice. There has been acceptance and rejection. If it is to function at all, culture can only function within the limits designed by its system, its grid. Therefore all culture must needs be a partial truth.

Lautréamont rejects culture and opts for nature, for him, the place of unrestricted being, the place beyond either–or, where you can both have your cake and eat it. *Les Chants* render the image of nature through the combination of the motifs of the circle and the straight line. The specific significance of these figures emerges in what is perhaps the most important passage of the book. It provides an image which it describes as the image of nature, executing a movement that is itself a combination of circle and straight line; a synthesis that overrides all partial truths, all contradictions. The passage ostensibly describes the flight of starlings:

> *Oh, what an abundant source of errors and mistakes is all partial truth!* Flocks of starlings have a way of flying that is peculiar to them, and seems to be subject to uniform and regular tactics, as would be a disciplined body obeying the voice of a single leader. *It is the voice of instinct that starlings obey*, and their instinct impels them to draw ever nearer to the centre of the troop, whilst the speed of their flight drives them ever outward; thus this multitude of birds, united in their common tendency to be drawn toward the same point, coming and going ceaselessly, turning and passing each other in every direction, forms a kind of violently agitated whirlwind, the total mass of which, following no definite direction, seems to have a general motion of rotation about its own axis, which results from the individual turning movement of each of its parts, whereby the centre, perpetually tending to expand, but always under pressure, is forced back in by the opposing effort of the surrounding lines, which are similarly treated as they approach the centre.[2]

The passage indicates the significance of the *tourbillon* and its eventual transformation into Mervyn and Maldoror. The movement is an image of totality, in that it is a combination of pointless circularity and purposive linear progress. Moreover, the whirling band of starlings is a disciplined body without a head. They are naturally ordered and purposeful; but no choice has limited the scope of their purpose. They are the image of nature itself. The image describes the place to which the poet aspires: a mode of being beyond culture, contradictions and partial truths. He can only move towards it by breaking down culture itself.

His first prerequisite must be a constant vigilance. It is when we are sleeping, when we are not thinking, that we find ourselves taking things for granted. Culture infiltrates us when we are not looking. It is then that 'our door is open to the fierce curiosity of the Celestial Bandit'.[3] But Maldoror has no intention of letting his security be breached: 'The white catacomb of my intelligence will never open its sanctuaries to the eye of the Creator.'[4] This is why he has not slept in twenty years, and why he remains unchanging. This state of perpetual mental tension is echoed by his physical appearance: 'My member always offers the mournful spectacle of turgescence; no one can boast that he has seen it in a state of normal repose.'[5] The constant sexual concentration is further equated with the state of mental awareness when it is suggested that he who sleeps is worse than impotent:

'He who sleeps is less than an animal castrated the day before.'[6]

Along with perpetual alertness and clarity of mind, it is mathematics that will be his major resource. He invokes them in a long lyrical hymn to *Mathématiques sévères*. Like logic and consciousness, they too are described as unchanging: 'You are always the same. No change, no foul air, brushes against the steep rocks and immense valleys of your identity.'[7] We are again in the *régime diurne* with images of hardness, clarity and the opposition of pure to impure. Mathematics moreover offer 'an extreme coldness, a consummate prudence and an implacable logic'.[8] Not only are they the source of Maldoror's aloofness, they are also the foundation of Lautréamont's absurd but logical humour, of his *pince-sans-rire* manner, indeed of his whole approach to literature: based on the creation of scenes with inner coherence, which seem totally absurd if matched against reality. It is no coincidence that the author of *Alice in Wonderland* was a mathematician.

In so far as mathematics created Lautréamont out of Ducasse, they may be thought of as having given birth to him, mothering him. Hence he writes of the 'aid of [their] fortifying milk'.[9] They represent an instrument with which he hopes to reach the truth because they are a discipline that generates its own development, regardless of whether or not what is developed seems reasonable, i.e. makes cultural sense. They are capable, as he writes, of re-expressing the entire world as a theorem; they can consider the world in terms of their own making as opposed to terms that have been made for us.

'Making sense' for Lautréamont is a value that is culture-bound. If we are to pass beyond the confines of our culture we must listen not to sense, but to reason.

If 'the absurd' proves such an effective means of demolishing our culture, it is because that culture sets the 'sensible' on a pedestal. To be told that something does not make sense is to be told to disregard it. The culture comes to demand sense, to be told what sense is, and to have sense fed to it as a pre-digested pabulum.

This process of pre-digestion is to be found in popular and not-so-popular criticism. The critic shares with his public the premise that somewhere, well hidden in the bowels of every work of art, is a hidden treasure—its sense. The unenlightened cannot hope to find it alone, any more than the people of Israel could hear the voice of the Lord without the mediation of a prophet. It is the prophet-critic who knows how to find the *deus absconditus*, the true meaning of the work of art. If we obey his instructions he will lead us to it. We disregard him at our extreme peril. If we do so, and attempt to tackle the work unaided, we will almost certainly miss the point, and this, *by definition*, will make our journey useless.

It has been argued that Ducasse's assault on God, as the fountainhead of all kinds of authority, is an assault on the interpretational approach to art, an approach that suggests there is such a thing as the true sense of a work of art, and that certain privileged persons have monopoly rights over it.

This is a view that has its devotees among the great critics of our time. Who cannot recall one or other of the great names of contemporary criticism telling us, in a televised lecture with live lantern slides, precisely why Rembrandt was a truly great artist, while there is some doubt about the actual greatness of Raphael? These high priests of civilisation speak with an authority that brooks no contradiction. They *know*, and if we disagree, they greet that disagreement with a smile, because the Lord knows how foolish these mortals can be.

Fortunately the apparatus of criticism and scholarship, the machinery of sense, is forever with us to tell us what we ought to like. Anyone who has been submitted to the indignity of a searching interview with a high priest of the liberal tradition will know this to his cost. The priesthood is beautifully described in *Getting Straight*. An otherwise indifferent movie, it contains a superb *viva voce* sequence, in which the hero fails his master's degree. He goes berserk when he realises that he will only pass, and thereby acquire the right to become a teacher himself, if he recognises that his examiner has his own monopoly on the truth—a monopoly that requires any candidate who faces him to concede that Scott Fitzgerald was queer.

This scene should not be dismissed lightly. It is an excellent account of a ritual common to all societies: the rites of passage. In order to qualify as a member of the inner circle of educators, the hero, acted by Elliott Gould, has to show that he accepts the principle on which the inner circle is founded; the principle of authoritarian monopoly on true meaning. He has to admit that if he failed to recognise that Fitzgerald was a homosexual, his whole reading of *Gatsby* must be wrong *by definition*. Only if he is prepared to stomach this kind of institutionalised absurdity can he qualify as an educator, for the defence of the monopoly is what education is about. It will be recalled that Jules Henry referred to school as the place in which you learn to be absurd.

Lautréamont assaults sense for the same reason that he assaults law and order. Sense, being God-given, is part of the big lie. Rather than read his book sensibly, he begs us to read it carefully and logically: not the same thing. The reader will get lost 'unless he bring to bear, when reading, rigorous logic and a mental tension that is at least the equal of his mistrust'.[10] Elsewhere he writes: 'I warn him who reads me to beware of forming a vague, and hence false, conception of the literary beauties I produce, in the excessively rapid development of my sentences.'[11] We are asked to read him with a mind that is open, not culture-bound. Only in this way will his readers persist with passages that are logical but absurd. We should trust logic, not sense, because logic is uncontaminated, whereas the instinct that makes us reject certain propositions as absurd is really the voice of the censor. It is by allowing logic to take us beyond the limits of sense that we will beat him.

The book takes us well beyond the pale of received values with its use of the pornography of violence. Our natural capacity to wallow in violence is an aspect of our being that is culturally taboo, deemed not to exist. Yet its existence is confirmed repeatedly by the role that sublimated violence plays on every level of our culture, from blood-sports to Italian Westerns.

This is a truth which we only face with difficulty; a difficulty we can measure by our attitude to the most troubling figure of our civilisation, the divine Marquis de Sade. De Sade is the very symbol of cultural taboo. This is not just because he is dirty, but because, in a manner strikingly close to that of Lautréamont, he sets out to destroy the very principles on which our society is founded: law and order, cause and effect—the universe that our culture has created for us with God at its head.

De Sade and Lautréamont resemble each other in their thoughts and in their pleasures. Lautréamont certainly situates his eroticism on an axis of pain, and the following lines of de Sade are quite reminiscent of Maldoror's dream of torturing, and then consoling, an adolescent. One of de Sade's heroes, Noirceuil, is advising Juliette how to treat a girl placed in her trust:

> What I should do in your place would be to amuse myself as much as I wanted with this girl, and steal her fortune, then place her in such an unhappy position that you can at every moment increase your happiness by the charms of watching her languish; as far as pleasure is concerned that will be better than killing her. The happiness I recommend will be far stronger; for you will have both the physical satisfaction of the pleasures you have had with her and the intellectual satisfaction of comparing her lot with your own.[12]

De Sade's thought also matches that of Lautréamont.

Although his views on nature are not consistent, he sets up truth to nature as his way of living authentically—as did most of the thinkers of his time. He differs from them in that his nature is infinitely red in tooth and claw. Culture is, for him, a distortion, a frustration of natural instinct, and, for him, the embodiment of culture is God.

De Sade considers that man has made God in his own image: cruel, treacherous and hypocritical. The Christian society, the place of causality and legal sanction, shapes a highly distorted world-view, which relies on the trinity of God, Law and Conscience to cheat us by stifling the legitimate voice of desire. It sublimates desire by transference: the trinity is eroticised to take the place of natural desire. We find another echo of Genet here, with his overt eroticisation of the machinery of justice, crime and punishment.

De Sade is very aware of the erotic obscenity of the machinery of law and order:

> In all ages man has enjoyed spilling the blood of his fellows and, in order to assuage his passion, he sometimes disguised it beneath the veil of justice, sometimes beneath that of religion. But basically his purpose was, without any doubt, the astonishing pleasure that it gave him.[13]

De Sade suggests that society's executive officers, the gentlemen so well portrayed by Bacon's portraits of cardinals in butchers' shops, deceive both us and themselves when they use the argument that 'this is going to hurt me more than it will hurt you'. According to de Sade, God and religion are mere excuses that we manufacture in order to justify, and practise, human iniquity. Perhaps the Grand Inquisitor was happy in his work. De Sade goes on to assault the metaphysics of his culture, suggesting that the very concept of a planned and balanced universe is part of the big lie. We are no more dependent on God than we are on Nature, and cause may well be irrelevant to effect.

Such statements taken into conjunction with *Les Chants* form a composite picture which suggests that God, Law, Conscience, Cause, Nature itself, are mere products of the culture-pattern; they are unreal, culture-bound. As partial truths they are only true in so far as they constitute a mediated sublimation of our repressed desires; they are partial in that desire must be re-coded into the language of crime and punishment in order to be accepted. This is why, in the world of Dostoevsky and of Kafka, no punishment is complete without the acquiescence of the victim. This is why Maldoror's murderees do not struggle.

Lautréamont and de Sade both champion the cause of cold reason in the midst of wild but always reflective excess. Their fantasies are the product of their intellect. Lautréamont derives his sense of the absurd from mathematics. The postures, actions and permutations of de Sade's eroticism are also visibly the product of a deductive rationalism pushed well beyond the threshold of absurdity; a wild, chilled mathematician's theorem, an experiment in sexual topology.

It is this emphasis on cold reason that accounts for the name of one of de Sade's most demonic creations. *Juliette* describes the initiation of the eponymous heroine at the hands of a liberated English lady named Clairwil, or clear will. Like Maldoror, her rigorous mind takes her into the world of the absurd. We are invited to employ reason in the liberation of the self, bursting through the restrictive bonds of an inherited world-view that informs us that the world is a place of law, sense and causality.

De Sade invites us to step outside the culture-pattern and start thinking for ourselves. He outdoes Lautréamont himself with the suggestion that the very concept of nature is itself culture-bound. He regards the nature–culture distinction as the product of a culture which always adheres to the pattern of meaning arrived at through choice—either/or. Like Lautréamont he relies on pure consciousness to achieve the triumph of will. Clairwil, like Maldoror, wishes to bring the universe of order crashing down about our ears. Just as Maldoror never sleeps, so Clairwil wishes her activity to transcend the petty distinctions between sleeping and waking, and even life and death:

> I would like to find a crime the perpetual workings of which would function even when I shall no longer, so that there would not be a single moment of my life, during which, even asleep, I would not be the cause of some disorder, so that this disorder would spread to the point when it would bring

about such universal corruption, such basic derangement, that the effect would be prolonged well beyond the span of my life.[14]

Another fascinating affinity between the two authors is the role played in their works by incest. Incest, which is de Sade's supreme channel of erotic communication, also plays a vital role in *Les Chants*. This is very important. We have suggested somewhat tentatively that incest taboo and language are the only two universal features of human society. The intensity of the incest taboo, and the degree of kinship prohibited, can vary, and exceptions can be made in special cases such as royal families. But some restriction or other would appear to be common to all human societies. Now it seems possible that incest taboo and language derive from the same kind of mental capacity. In order to be able to conceive of incest as an interdiction, it is necessary to be able to conceive of kinship links. This requires one to think of people not only as human objects, but in terms of their symbolic roles. This in turn presupposes a capacity to situate individual elements in the framework of a general structure, with its categories of similarity and difference, like and unlike, near and remote, related and unrelated. In order to be able to conceive of relations of kinship, *one has to be able to think symbolically*, to have a capacity to reach a level of abstraction on which people are conceived of as signs. Is it not precisely the same ability that permits us to use sounds symbolically and turn *them* into signs? In both cases, whether it be human objects, or the sounds of language, it is necessary that these be conceived of in terms of what they represent as opposed to what they are.

Language would therefore seem to be associated with the imposition of taboo and interdiction. Together with the incest taboo it lies at the very heart of the cultural principle, and is associated, in some not very precise sense, with the imposition of restraint upon desire.

It is through language that we operate the grid that parcels the world into sets and categories. It thereby creates its own set of taboos. Because it is by definition a partial truth, it is obliged to exclude and disregard whole areas of potential experience, which it must classify as noise and treat as unsayable, beyond the pale, taboo.

The association of incest with the very principle of social man's self-awareness is embodied in the Oedipus myth. For Lévi-Strauss, the Oedipus cycle consists of myths forming binary oppositions, such as incest–parricide, that represent the over- and under-valuing of kinship relations. It is only through a balanced interpretation of kinship that human society can be founded. Equally it might be said that Oedipus, through the self-inflicted punishment of his incest, discovers the very principle of taboo and transgression. But he also discovers the principles of self-knowledge and understanding, indeed of language itself. For he is the great cryptographer, able to solve the riddle of the sphinx, and discover that the answer is 'man'. He achieves self-consciousness because he *possesses the capacity to think symbolically.* Quite intuitively, the myth seems to have found an archetypal link between the awareness of incest and the very principle of understanding.[15]

Infringement of the incest taboo is crucial to the work of both Lautréamont and de Sade, because it represents the infringement of the principle of partial truth itself; that principle which makes culture possible.

Incest manifests itself in various ways in *Les Chants*, and is part of a larger enterprise, also shared by de Sade, namely the disruption of kinship. Maldoror's ambition is to destroy the family, for such destruction is tantamount to the destruction of the social instinct: 'I have made a pact with prostitution in order to sow disorder in families.'[16]

Ducasse seems to have experienced such disruption at first hand. He was sent away from home, at an early age, to a strange country thousands of miles away. It may well have been this traumatic experience, the realisation of what parents are capable of doing to their children 'for their own good', that made him see the paternalistic, authoritarian structure of his society as a gigantic confidence trick. This would explain the intensity of feeling with which he writes of family ties:

The great universal family of man is a utopia worthy of the most mediocre logic ... one immediately recalls all those parents ungrateful enough towards the Creator to abandon the fruit of their wretched union.[17]

Such attitudes make the family relations of *Les Chants* somewhat intense. The family is an imprisoning bond, and becomes an image for society itself. Imposing restraint upon desire, it is described as 'the triple fetter that enslaved me'.[18]

Strange things happen within the bosom of a family. Fratricide is not unusual. Witness the story of the web-footed swimmer, who has forsaken human form and taken to the water, as the result of an unfortunate experience. His brother turned his parents against him, and they shut him up for fifteen years,

> with grubs and muddy water as my only sustenance ... Sometimes, in the course of the day, one of the three torturers would take his turn to enter laden with pincers and various instruments. The cries their tortures tore from me left them unmoved; the abundant loss of my blood made them smile.[19]

Kinship and relations between siblings are regularly rendered in terms of violence and murder: 'I extended to him the hand with which the fratricide murdered his sister.'[20] Lautréamont reserves his most extreme distortions of conventional relationships for the bond between parent and child. This is described in terms of torture or lust. Maldoror's own relations with his victims are termed paternal. The author suggests that what passes for education is merely the parents' attempt to force their children into their own wretched mould. Lautréamont implies that the business of education is to form the child in the image of the father, ensuring that the latter will not go to hell unaccompanied. Hence the irony of such expressions as: 'I seem to be talking in a manner that is deliberately paternal, so that humanity has no cause for complaint.'[21] The mother is treated no more generously. She is described as being dry of milk—in contrast to the fortifying milk of mathematics. He writes of sucking 'the dry dugs of what is known as a mother'.[22] Mothers do not always respect the spark of life in their offspring: 'Feed it a newly-born bastard whose mother wants it to die.'[23]

When they are not expressed in terms of hate, the relations of kinship are rendered through lust. This represents the sundering of family ties. A member of your family, and hence the same as you, is converted into the object of your lust, and hence becomes different from you.

If the family is to be kept together, a father must command respect. Otherwise his son will become his sexual rival: 'otherwise ... they will advance with great strides, driven by revolt against the day of their birth and the clitoris of their impure mother.'[24] Eroticisation of the mother, who cannot be conceived of at one time as both a mother and a sexual object, is associated with revolt against parental authority. The infant revolutionary symbolises the revolt of an entire generation, 'its strong fist raised against heaven, like that of a child already nourishing perverse thoughts about its mother'.[25] Lautréamont encourages us to seek liberation by cutting our mother's arms off. Failing a mother, a sister will serve.

The work also treats incest directly. Maldoror has an incestuous coupling. After observing a shipwreck—it will be recalled that he dispatched the sole survivor—he swims out to sea to join a huge female shark, and makes love to her:

> Two sinewy thighs gripped the viscous skin of the monster closely, like two leeches; arms and fins entwined themselves lovingly around the body of the loved one, as their throats and breasts came to form a single glaucous mass that reeked of seaweed; in the midst of the storm that raged on; in the lightning's flash; with foaming waves for their marriage bed, carried on an undersea current as if in a cradle, rolling down to unknown depths of the abyss, they were joined in a coupling long, chaste and hideous.[26]

The coupling is imagined as incestuous. The episode began with Maldoror looking for someone that resembled him, and finding the shark. Sex is expressed in a language of similarity. They make love in the sea, and the homophony of *mère* and *mer* is not to be disregarded, the more so since they make love in a cradle. Maldoror, moreover, dreams of having a shark for a mother: 'I would rather have been the son of the female shark whose hunger is the friend of storms.'[27]

Inversion of family relations is brought to a peak when Maldoror comes upon the man strung up by his hair. He is being diligently beaten by his wife and mother. His mother wished to sleep with him, and had promised her daughter-in-law a large sum of money if she succeeded. She summoned him to her room one evening and 'ordered him to undress, in order to pass the night with her in a bed, and without awaiting an answer, maternity divested herself of her garments, whilst executing the most lubricious gestures'.[28] The expression *maternity* emphasises the incest theme. On the son's refusal the women grow so angry that they string him up and talk as they beat him : ' "You have a firm hold on life oh my beloved husband . . ." "Why don't you die oh my gracious son?" '[29] The passage represents the final transgression of all limits, all verisimilitude: verisimilitude is itself a limit. It is beyond comprehension, its very existence a contradiction in cultural terms.

The author's explicit refusal to adopt an anthropocentric world-view, whereby man is the lord of creation, is yet another of his attempts to shake us out of our culture-pattern. He tries to destroy the humanist perspective, in the full sense of that word. His anti-human tendency drives another crack into the façade of Western culture.

One of that culture's unwritten laws is that the world is ordered according to a certain hierarchy. This places the civilised European at its summit, descends through Jews and Orientals to Arabs, thence to Indians, heathenish and idolatrous Africans, Amerindians, thoroughbred horses, and pedigree dogs, aborigines and other remnants of Stone Age culture to wild animals, trees, plants and minerals. A hierarchy of this kind forms the corner-stone of WASP culture. Thus the events of My Lai would have been inconceivable, would have seemed like war-crimes, in anything but a Third World context. In Vietnam they were simply the flash-point in a public-relations crisis for the military. War-crimes are atrocities perpetrated by the other side, and our boys would never gun down innocent Caucasian women and children. An analysis of the way in which the military in South-East Asia form their categories of similarity and difference would simply show that humanity is a relative concept and that 'gooks' are not quite human.

Lautréamont has no truck with any such hierarchy. His anti-humanism accounts for the plethora of different species of animal—over a hundred—that we find in *Les Chants*. He seeks to place man in his cultural and physical environment without the benefit of a humanist classification. Just as he declines to write a book that will simply be a projection of the author's viewpoint, so he declines to accept the privileged situation which culture has accorded to man.

His rhetoric tries to de-humanise man, to break down the privileged distinction between human and non-human. Hence the metamorphoses of Dazet, and the ease with which Maldoror changes shape. There is nothing privileged or binding about the human form. Indeed, it has associations one may wish to avoid. The man who has been tortured for fifteen years is disgusted with his fellows 'who although they called themselves my fellows did not appear to resemble me in any way'.[30] Therefore he changes his shape and takes to the sea, determined never to touch land again. His rejection of humanity is complete: 'broad duck's feet in the place of hands and feet, carrying a dorsal fin, proportionately as long and pointed as that of a dolphin'.[31] He is accompanied by fish that bear him 'the most obvious marks of great admiration'.[32] The rejection of the human point of view explains the role of animals in this book. For example the author illustrates the principles of *Les Chants* with the flight of starlings, because animals are essentially innocent. One of poetry's chief virtues for Lautréamont is that it is essentially anti-human, and free from cultural contamination: 'You should know that poetry is to be found wherever the stupid mocking smile of duck-faced man is absent.'[33]

In passages such as these the author seems to have grasped the idea which we are only slowly coming to understand, namely that there is nothing special about Western civilisation. Indeed one would be entitled to see in it the greatest source of destruction, the greatest entropic force, that this world has so far seen.

CHAPTER FOURTEEN

Beyond Similarity and Difference

In our study of *Les Chants* we have, ourselves, been obliged to follow the pattern of the *tourbillon*. We began on the outside, by discussing the work's superficial qualities: surface-structure phenomena such as references to the popular novel, and black humour. Gradually we have worked our way to the centre, and have now arrived there: at the kernel, the core of meaning which has shaped the entire work. It is of course no coincidence that we should have followed the pattern of *Les Chants,* but neither was it the consequence of an *a priori* choice on the part of the author. This matching of critical approach to the pattern of Lautréamont's own thought shows how strongly formed his writing is.

One of the most searching questions that one can ask of one's response to a writer is: have you read him at your pace or at his? The writer must seek to gain a hold over his readers, that obliges them to read him in his way, and prevents them from using him as they please. Not only are we obliged to read Lautréamont in his way, we are even obliged to write and think about him in his way. If we are to hope to echo and amplify his thought without distortions, we must follow the pattern of the *tourbillon*. This sense of obligation is the most telling proof of the coherence, complexity and sheer strength of the text: the system he has put together so carefully out of words.

Lautréamont's aversion to partial truths, situations containing an inherent obligation to make a choice—to be *either* a classical *or* a romantic artist—is reflected in his view of his own work. He does not see himself in the main line of Western art, which is based on perpetual self-renewal, whereby one form loses its vitality only to be superseded by another. He rejects this linear model, which strings each masterpiece like a pearl onto the thread of history. His work belongs to one side of tradition. He refuses to take up the running, to carry the baton

142

for a moment in the perpetual relay race of literary history. He has greater ambitions. As an artist who seeks for the overthrow of all cultural barriers, the reassessment of all values, he has no interest in transitory cultural kudos; he wants absolutes. Although inevitably part of his culture, he hopes that his work will transcend partial truth.

> [My intention is] to invent a poetry completely outside the normal progress of nature, the corrupting breath of which will appear to overwhelm the most absolute of truths.
>
> Perhaps this simple ideal conceived by my imagination will surpass all the most grandiose and sacred of poetry's inventions to date.
>
> Till now, poetry took the wrong road; rising up to heaven or grovelling on the ground, it failed to recognise the principles of its existence . . . It has not been modest.[1]

Lautréamont has the highest expectations of his work; not because of its execution, but because of its basis. This is why it is no distortion of *Les Chants* to use it to illuminate our own cultural predicament: it is a research tool designed to make its readers ask themselves questions. It is quite unlike traditional poetry, whatever its quality, because poetry tends to be concerned with self-expression or, at the very least, with the expression of a single viewpoint. Before Lautréamont literature concerned itself with partial truths, truths both limited and partisan. His approach is different; rather than take sides he shows us how it comes about that sides are taken. He distinguishes his work from traditional poetry which invariably concerned itself with the transcendence of particular limits— parish-pump extremism. Such poetry was over-ambitious and hence ineffective. The kind of poetry that moves only in a single direction cannot avoid partial truth.

Lautréamont begs us to recognise that he is attempting something different. We must beware of interpreting his work through the focus of cultural stereotypes. We must read him without prejudice if we are to understand him:

> It would be dangerous to impart a narrow and false interpretation to an eminently philosophical conception which ceases

to be rational, once it is no longer understood as it was conceived, that is to say generously.[2]

The author begs us to read him with open minds, to use our powers of deductive reason, rather than the series of ready-made attitudes of acceptance and rejection, which we allow to function as the apparatus of judgment because we are too lazy to treat each particular case on its own merits.

If we read Lautréamont as we would a poet of the nineteenth century, the result is chaos; a world of absurd and meaningless violence, undisciplined lyricism and the occasional anticipation of surrealism. But what appear, at first sight, to be the ravings of a deranged mind, look very different if we use our reason, not our prejudices, to read Lautréamont. Then we find that our criteria are formed by structuralism, Lévi-Strauss, linguistics, McLuhan, Marcuse, and all the modish reference points of our own culture, which combine to turn Lautréamont into a 'modern master'.

Whatever his reservations, the reader must at least, suggests Lautréamont, try to free himself from his own condition of partial truth, and concede that there might be more to Lautréamont than he can see at first sight. This admission is the first step towards eventual liberation. The reader need only concede that Lautréamont's approach is:

> within the bounds of possibility. There is no doubt that between the two extremes of literature, as you understand it, and as I do, there is an infinite range of alternatives.[3]

He asks us to stretch our minds and throw out everything that helps to form cultural stereotypes, that makes us think about new things in terms of old experiences.

Like Marx, he suggests that what passes for a personal set of values is really the product of circumstance. But, unlike Marx, he believes in the innocence of pure reason. Reason, logic and mathematics cannot be contaminated by culture. A capitalist form of logic is no more possible than a Marxist-Leninist form of chess—it may be the political and cultural neutrality of chess that makes it so popular in countries which do not encourage politico-cultural heterodoxy. In so far as man fails to apply these uncontaminated skills to the business of self-liberation, he is

narrow, limited and a victim to partial truth. Man is therefore
described in a language of restriction. We are 'men with
narrow shoulders'.[4] Yet we retain a lingering intuitive sense that
a liberated existence is possible beyond the confines of the cell.
We all want to break free: 'They thirst for infinity like you,
like me, like the rest of mankind with its pale long face.'[5] This
latent intuition is a potential basis for a Promethean broadening
of our psyche: 'man by virtue of his complex and multiple
nature knows how to broaden its frontiers'.[6] Since we are
complex and multiple, capable of self-contradiction and
revisionism, we are capable of grasping the absurdity of a
fixed viewpoint—the very incarnation of partial truth. The
classic manifestation of a complex and multiple nature is of
course the mutual contradiction of *Les Chants* and *Poésies*.

One of the ways in which the author seeks to broaden our
frontiers is by means of arguments that reduce a proposition
to absurdity. He tries to make us think thoughts that appear
unthinkable. It is by continually compelling ourselves to think
the unthinkable that we may build up our mental muscles and
flex our minds in such a way that they broaden.

The most obvious way in which Lautréamont works on our
minds, and forces us to discard our stereotypes, is his re-writing
of the rules of poetic rhetoric. His style is extreme in every
respect. The style of *Poésies* is banal to the point of tedium, the
banality of minimal art; that of *Les Chants* is so full of
extravagance that it takes on extraordinary uniformity. The
two works are so unlike that they seem identical. It is the scale
of their extremism that we recognise, not their respective
characteristics. Where *Poésies* describes school-speechday prizes
as the height of Western literary achievement, *Les Chants*
exemplifies its idea of beauty with a series of images. They form
the most characteristic paradigm of the whole book, the paradigm of *As beautiful as* . . . , a set of images that oblige one to
re-think one's conception of beauty, poetry, comparison and
finally language itself. It includes such items as:

> he appeared to me as beautiful as the two long antennae
> of an insect; or rather, like a hasty burial . . . but above all,
> like an eminently putrescent liquid.[7]

Another passage describes someone as beautiful as:

145

the retractability of the talons of birds of prey; or like the uncertain muscular movements in wounds in the soft part of the posterior cervical region; or rather like the perpetual rat-trap, always re-set by the animal it has caught, which can capture rodents indefinitely, functioning even when hidden under straw; and above all, like a sewing-machine and an umbrella meeting by chance on a dissecting table![8]

The last image was a favourite of the surrealists. It is strangely reminiscent of the work of Max Ernst, Duchamp or Man Ray. With its emphasis on the angular products of the machine age that have a sinister life of their own, it is very much an image created by a society geared up to mass-production, and marketing. The rat-trap could well have been borrowed directly from advertising copy, whereas the visual impression of the last image is strangely reminiscent of nineteenth-century mail-order catalogues.

The final example of this paradigm is also the strangest:

As beautiful as the congenital fault in the conformation of man's sexual organs, whereby the urethral canal is short, its lower wall divided or absent, with the result that the channel opens at a variable distance below the glans, and on the underside of the penis; or like the fat conical wattle, lined with transverse creases, which rises from the base of the upper beak of the turkey.[9]

Such sequences are clearly the product of fold-in techniques, the incorporation of sources such as sales literature and medical dictionaries. But the actual sources are not important, what matters is the transformations brought about.[10]

The author is mounting an attack on the concept of beauty. He shows us that it is possible to put anything and everything after a phrase beginning 'As beautiful as ...'. He thereby liberates us from a particular partial truth that states that certain elements may be appropriately linked together in a particular syntagmatic relationship, whereas the linking of any other elements would be unseemly.

By breaking down the distinction between beautiful and not-beautiful, Lautréamont blows apart the conventions of aesthetic propriety. He makes us realise that we will accept anything as being beautiful, provided it occurs in the right context.

No less important is his destruction of the convention that suggests that the imagination should be kept on a tight rein. Common sense and imagination would seem to have entered into a pact whereby imagination might lend spice to common sense, but *la folle du logis* must not go too far. The author derives some of his greatest mind-expanding resources from the infringement of this pact:

> The limit accorded by common sense to imagination is some-
> times, notwithstanding this brief truce concluded by these
> two powers, regrettably exceeded by the energetic forces of
> the will.[11]

Lautréamont violates the truce at every turn. It is in the interests of such mind-expanding violation that he introduces walk-on parts such as the adolescents 'who derive their pleasure from raping the corpses of beautiful women not long dead'.[12] He is not trying to shock us with this imagery, but to make us immune to the shock it produces. The freer we become from cultural stereotype and preconception, the more able we will be to judge for ourselves. Stepping outside the cultural stereo-type that condemns necrophilia absolutely, we can see that the practice is utterly innocent. It hurts no one, keeps the kids off the streets, and the victims are past complaining. Necrophilia may sound abhorrent, even when compared to conventional sex-crimes; in fact it is much less anti-social.

It is in the interests of mind-expansion that Maldoror is made to overstep the limits of humanity itself, in his coupling with the shark. He also makes love to a louse, and impregnates it:

> I slept with it for three successive nights and threw it into the
> ditch. Human fecundation, which would not have taken place
> in other such instances, was, on this particular occasion,
> accepted by fate.[13]

The world of *Les Chants* is a world of fluid frontiers and free-flowing forms. Categories of species and kind are not watertight—they hardly function. Angels turn into silver lamps and back again, or become crabs, Hope turns into a dragon, and Maldoror flits from form to form. This fluidity impresses upon us that our so-called inflexible categories are less rigid than they seem. It also has a deeper significance.

Anthropologists and students of mythology agree that one of the chief characteristics of the world of myth is metamorphosis. Ernst Cassirer writes:

> [In myth] there is no specific difference between the various realms of life. Nothing has a definite, invariable, static shape. By a sudden metamorphosis everything may be turned into everything. If there is any characteristic and outstanding feature of the mythical world, any law by which it is governed—it is this law of metamorphosis.[14]

In the world of myth, freedom to change one's shape represents freedom to escape from the confines of our particular earthly condition. Metamorphosis is one of the ways in which the imagination dreams of immortality and seeks to cheat death. Our body may rot, but we can either step outside it, or re-express that very rotting as a change, a metamorphosis.

Seen in the light of metamorphosis, Maldoror is the supreme mythic hero. In his final ritual ascent he achieves a total transcendence and triumph over his mortality. Metamorphosis is his supreme source of delight. 'Metamorphosis always appeared to me as the greatest and most resounding echo of perfect bliss.'[15] This view contrasts very strongly with the way metamorphosis is regarded by Gogol or Kafka. Where Lautréamont advocates the destruction of every kind of existing order, they experience the possibility of such breakdown with anguish. Things are falling apart, the world gradually losing its stability. Hence both writers treat metamorphosis as an anxiety motif, not the source of delight it is for Lautréamont, who sees it as a means of escape from the narrow confines of the human context.

This urge to dissolve all hide-bound forms and categories constitutes the essential motivation of the assault on kinship and the family. The poet makes a literal nonsense of the relationships between son, mother and daughter-in-law. Incest and violence within the family's bosom represent the transgression of all forms of limitation and taboo. Other aspects of the work take this process even further. Being physically possible, nothing about incest goes against physical nature. By terming it a taboo we classify it as the product of culture. Lautréamont takes

his mind-bending a stage further, and goes against nature itself.
He confronts us with sets of relationships which constitute contradictions in natural terms. We find a bird and a beetle related
—they are brothers! But the author goes well beyond such crude
contradictions. If nature is the place beyond contradiction, in
which you can both have and eat your cake, then Maldoror
is 'naturally' related to the brother of the three Marguerites,
as he multiplies both sex and identity: 'The three Marguerites
will re-live in me and what's more I shall be your mother.'[16]

The theme of homosexuality is also part of the paradigm of
the transgression of limits. In his long invocation to the
'pédérastes incompréhensibles' the author finds them interesting
precisely because they are outsiders, ghetto-dwellers beyond the
understanding of the straight world. Unlike the straight they
think of sexuality in terms not of difference, but similarity.
Endogamous to the point of auto-eroticism, they enjoy a degree
of self-sufficiency that the straight world can never know. The
definitive imaginative treatment of this sexual dream is the
gentle and totally self-sufficient hermaphrodite:

> There in a grove surrounded by flowers sleeps the herm-
> aphrodite on grass drenched with his tears. The moon's disc
> has moved clear of the clouds, and its pale beams caress this
> smooth adolescent face. His features display the most manly
> energy together with the celestial grace of a madonna.
> Nothing appears natural in him, not even his muscles that
> thread through the harmonious contours of his feminine form.
> He has one arm bent across his brow, the other hand rests
> upon his breast, as if to check the beating of a heart cut off
> from all confidences, and laden with the weighty burden of
> an eternal secret. Tired of life, and ashamed of passing thus
> among beings that do not resemble him, despair has taken
> possession of his soul, and he walks alone, like the beggar of
> the valley.[17]

The hermaphrodite only appears briefly. The pederasts are
accorded more space. They possess 'a sixth sense which we lack'.
They pass beyond our limits, combining opposing forms of
sheer extremism:

> Your prostitution is available to the first comer and tests the

149

logic of the profoundest thinkers, whereas your exaggerated sensibilities are a source of overwhelming wonder to woman herself.[18]

The utter instant promiscuity of the homosexual lifestyle is quite incomprehensible to those of us who think of cottages as small thatched residences in the country. It is one of the components of utter paradox, when it is combined with the highly developed delicacy of feeling with which it can go hand in hand. Pederasts are yet another contradiction in cultural terms.

With the notion of contradiction in terms we have arrived at the centre of the work. Culture is the product of the operation of a finite series of choices functioning across the grid of similarity and difference, inclusion and exclusion, *cliché* and *taboo*. It is these terms that make language and symbolic representation possible; our sense of like and unlike that renders our environment meaningful. We have to know the name of whatever we will be looking at, in order to be able to see it. The unknown must be matched against the known before it can be handled.

The psychologist William James has suggested that the infant would find the world about him a 'buzzing, blooming confusion'. It is only gradually that this becomes classified and ordered. But as we mature we merely explore the border-lands of the unknown, and this in terms of what we know already. Strangeness, i.e. difference, must be re-classified as similarity, before it can be expressed. When required to depict a rhinoceros, an animal he had never seen, the artist Dürer expressed his vision in terms of familiar schemata, using the form of a dragon, with an armoured body. We can only know at all by using this process of matching and categorisation that creates working approximations. This is why language is ludicrously inadequate. It will always betray us by creating an approximation of our meaning, and will never serve us faithfully. Language cheats us all.

Were we able to liberate ourselves from the partial truths of symbolic representation, break down the noise–signal distinction once and for all, our environment would collapse into a single unstructured continuum. All sense of time, identity and distinction would disappear. The sense of law, the reality principle, the arguments of our insurance salesmen counselling prudence, who tell us to pay now and live later, would all switch off, and we would attain a state of plenitude beyond both pain and pleasure.

But unfortunately culture has us by the throat. Similarity and difference—or binary contrast—is utterly crucial to the working of language: de Saussure's meaning implies choice. It forms a grid from which there is no escape. But partial release may be gained from the knowledge that we are being manipulated by that system, and from the understanding of how that manipulation comes about.

Lautréamont writes to teach us about manipulation, about the code in which we think. *Les Chants/Poésies,* Good/Evil, Man/Animal, Nature/Culture, the series of oppositions he unfolds for us have a vital symbolic function. They represent the way in which our minds work, represent our culture, our mental formation, our very selves. They offer a description of the conditions of contrast and binary choice that must obtain if thought is to function at all.

Although Lautréamont treats this topic indirectly, it is clearly this, the most restrictive of all our restrictions, that he is challenging. The paradigm of 'As beautiful as . . .' was designed to destroy our tendency to think in terms of 'Beautiful' or 'Not beautiful'. He creates a context so arbitrary that anything could occur in it. Consequently, in Saussurian terms, what follows 'As . . .' is no longer the consequence of choice, but random. This destroys the statement's capacity to have meaning. The paradigm is an assault on the picture of reality drawn for us by the grid. It seeks to destroy that picture by going beyond meaning itself.

A more specific attack on the categories of similarity and difference is to be found in the following sophisticated and sophistic parody of logical argument. The passage exposes the arbitrary way in which linguistic categories establish a sense of like and unlike which is valid only with reference to its conventions, not with reference to non-linguistic reality—just as colour terms are only relevant to the culture-pattern that generates them. It is language that shapes our patterns, not reality. If our particular categories place two objects in the same class, we treat them as belonging together, regardless of their 'real' relationship. This passage makes this point. It renders the argument as confusing and complex as possible, in order to question the whole concept of argument, test its validity against our own experience, rather than take its code for granted :

> Two pillars which it was not difficult and still less possible to mistake for two baobabs appeared in the valley, larger than two pins. In fact they were two huge towers. And although two baobabs, at first sight, do not resemble two pins, or even two towers, however by means of a skilful use of the ligatures of wisdom, one might affirm, without fear of being wrong (for if this affirmation were accompanied by the slightest shred of fear it would no longer be an affirmation; although a single name describes these two mental phenomena that offer characteristics sufficiently distinct not to be confused lightly), that a baobab is not so different from a pillar, that comparison should be forbidden between these two forms, architectural or geometric, or one or the other, or neither one nor the other, or rather forms tall and massive. I have just found, I would not presume to claim the contrary, the epithets proper to the substantives pillar and baobab.[19]

The last sentence makes it clear that the author is talking about words, not things, about the way that language assembles its picture of reality. He is concerned with rhetorical comparison, not with the psychology of perception. The absurd quality of the discussion points to the arbitrary nature of the categories that language creates for us. He comes to the conclusion that language, our principal instrument for deciphering reality, is itself rooted in unreality, that perhaps its definitive characteristic is nonsense.

Antonin Artaud derives his own aesthetic of the absurd, *The Theatre of Cruelty*, from just such a recognition of the lack of relationship between language and reality:

> It must be admitted that everything about the purpose of an object, about the meaning or use of a natural form, is a matter of convention.
>
> When nature gave to a tree the form of a tree, it could equally well have given it the form of an animal or a hill, we would have thought *tree* when faced by the animal or the hill, and this would have done the trick.

It is accepted that pretty women have harmonious voices; if from the beginning of time all pretty women had greeted us with elephantine trumpetings, we would have joined the idea of trumpetings with the idea of pretty women, and part of our inner vision of the world would have been radically transformed.

You must understand therefore that poetry is anarchical in that it questions all relationships between objects and between form and meaning.[20]

In passages such as the one in which Lautréamont examines the machinery of comparison, and shows how convention relates sets of objects, trees, pins, towers, that are seldom found together in reality, he is exposing the mainsprings of language itself, showing us how meaning is created. Another of de Saussure's laws of language was 'L'arbitraire du signe', the lack of any necessary relationship between a sign and what it refers to. Lautréamont develops the argument to hint at the arbitrary nature of language itself.

It is his preoccupation with the birth and nature of meaning that motivates the vice and sadism of *Les Chants*. These extremes of evil form part of an illustration of how meaning is created, how it is generated by a series of binary oppositions, contrasts and antitheses. We can only conceive of the behaviour described in *Les Chants* as vicious and evil, in so far as we can contrast that behaviour with an opposing pattern which we think of as good:

If I have allowed my vices to appear in these pages it will only make people believe the more in the virtues that I illuminate there.[21]

This explains the relationship between *Les Chants* and *Poésies*. Each work can only be understood by contrasting it with the other. In order to place *Les Chants* in a meaningful context, we must be aware of the possibility of *Poésies*, and vice versa. By writing the second work, the author simply makes explicit the process that every reader must go through for himself, with every book, indeed with every word, that he reads. We can only identify what *is,* by isolating and contrasting it with what it is *not.* All communication rests upon the possibility of choice and contrast; selection from a series of alternatives. Thus the two works represent two alternative extremes: *Poésies* are deliberately turned into everything *Les Chants* are not, and become their reverse image. They are signed Ducasse, their style is restrained and lapidary, with a tendency to pithy banality. They preach law and orthodoxy on every front, and are opposed to imaginative literature of any kind. In the words of their author:

I replace melancholy with courage, doubt with certainty, despair with hope, evil with good, complaint with duty, scepticism with faith, sophistry with the coldness of calm, pride with modesty.[22]

This is the reverse image of *Les Chants*. The author does not *mean* one more or less than the other. The opposing pair is the definitive illustration of the principle that meaning derives from choice, and that without choice there can be no meaning; no action without an equal and opposite reaction.

Maldoror seeks to escape from meaning's prison. It is our reflex-need to make sense of our experience that obliges us to divide and distinguish it, re-rendering it in terms of series of restrictive alternatives, hiving off noise from signal.

Maldoror teaches us to love nonsense. He is only attracted to creatures that resemble him: the only creature that resembles him is a huge female shark. Such a view of resemblance invalidates any possibility of ever talking about resemblance. It suggests that we cannot hope to dispose of classes and categories that have any real value, since the very idea of relationship is arbitrary. As Lautréamont writes: 'Perhaps when I suggest this I am wrong, but perhaps I am right.'[23] There is literally no knowing. Language simply creates an illusion of sense. The author lives in a world in which there is language but no meaning, phonemes but no semantemes: 'My years are few in number, and yet already I sense that goodness is no more than a group of sonorous syllables.'[24] But this is true not of *goodness* alone, but of every word in the lexicon. The relationship between words and things is quite arbitrary. Wittgenstein was much concerned with this question, and would ask what it might mean to say you 'hear' in a different sense the piano, its sound, the piece, the player and his fluency; to say that you marry in one sense a woman, in another her money.[25] The only common feature shared by these sets of actions is that they are described by the same word. They are no more related in reality than Maldoror and the shark. Lautréamont knows enough semantics to recognise that 'the same name expresses two mental phenomena that offer characteristics sufficiently distinct not to be readily confused'.[26] The author's refusal to divide or to distinguish is his recognition of language's failure to be meaningful, his refusal to be deluded by the dance of the categories, as they form and re-form in the shifting patterns of similarity and difference. He realises that this dance has nothing to do with anything but itself. *Les Chants* advocate the solution of total and unchanging identity, which overrides all distinctions between you and not-you; similarity and difference no longer operate. Once such contrastive attitudes have been overcome, you become the world, and the world becomes you. You achieve the ultimate objective, a unified brain which is impervious to the erosions of difference and antithesis:

> If I exist I am not another. I do not admit this equivocal plurality in myself. I wish to reside alone in the intimacy of my reasoning.[27]

The two images of perfection in this book, the sea and mathematics, both maintain an unchanging, uncontaminated identity. They remain unaltered and immune to the foul air of change and decay. The sea is the supreme image of unity and continuity, free from rupture of any kind:

> Old ocean, you are the symbol of identity, always equal to yourself . . . You are modest. Man perpetually congratulates himself on trifles. I salute you, old ocean.[28]

CHAPTER FIFTEEN

In Conclusion

... even if the individual has direct, personal experience of events, it is not really direct and primary: it is organised in stereotype. It takes long and skilful training to so uproot such stereotypes that an individual sees things freshly, in an unstereotyped manner. One might suppose, for example, that if all the people went through a depression they would all 'experience' it, and in terms of this experience, that they would all debunk or reject or at least refract what the media say about it ...

The kind of experience, in short, that might serve as a basis for resistance to mass media is not an experience of raw events, but the experience of meanings. The fleck of interpretation must be there in the experience if we are to use the word experience seriously. And the capacity for such experience is socially implanted. The individual does not trust his own experience ... until it is confirmed by others or by the media. Usually such direct exposure is not accepted if it disturbs loyalties and beliefs that the individual already holds. To be accepted, it must relieve or justify the feelings that often lie in the back of his mind as key features of his ideological loyalties.[1]

C. Wright Mills conveys to the intellect some of the insights that Lautréamont compels our emotions to acknowledge. He too teaches us that we work by stereotype and preconception. He tries to make us see things without the benefit of these aids, to teach us not to believe in the world-view that the media create.

Les Chants are designed to teach resistance to the media. They are concerned with the world of meanings and literature, not with the world of reality. They threaten our most deeply-rooted loyalties and beliefs, because they seek to make us do without them, just for a moment; to throw away our crutches and walk a few paces alone.

156

In Conclusion

Lautréamont is concerned first and last with the impact of the media on the individual consciousness, and with the nature of the distortions that they create. The fact that he wrote long before the creation of the global village should deceive no one. The poetry of Lautréamont is some of the most media-conscious work ever written. The electric media are, after all, only part of a much longer paradigm of symbolic systems that come between us and the world. Other forms of mediation would include kinship systems, and indeed language itself, the greatest mass medium of all. Appropriately then, our study of Lautréamont concludes with the examination of his treatment of his own medium, the written word.

This brings us to the true hero of the book, the person whom the poet wishes to bring to consciousness: the reader. The educational purpose of this book will be fulfilled in a phrase that the author imagines on the reader's lips: 'You must give him his due, he has largely cretinised me.'[2] His object is to use what Artaud described as the 'anarchy of poetry' to transform his readers from reasonable, hence culture-bound, creatures, into cultural outlaws, and hence, in the eyes of reasonable folk, into cretins.

The process of cretinisation functions on a number of levels, as the author tries to bring us to awareness without the benefit of our preconceptions. He exposes the nature of his own medium in the same way. He tells us how to handle the peculiar codes of *Les Chants,* taking us behind the scenes and showing us how they work.

It is a *sine qua non* of post-romantic literature that somewhere or other in the business of creation there is a mystery. This confers a special kind of privilege on the process of literary production. Everything that Lautréamont tells us about his own work refutes inspirationist theories of creativity. Lautréamont has no interest in the mystery of creation, in the whereabouts of the words before they reach the page. Instead he exposes the mystery which no other writer is prepared to reveal. Other artists, to a man, suggest that in one way or another, their work aims for a significance that transcends its status as an encoded message. They point to something of greater value, call it truth, sense, beauty, that is hidden in and around the words, but which one must pass beyond the words to

157

find. Lautréamont rejects this mystification. He wants us to know the truth; we are reading a text made of paper, words and nothing else. What we can see is all there is; the unfolding of language and its structural patterns. Poetry is no different from any other mode of discourse. It is, if anything, a science, not a religion. Lautréamont's concern to expose the myths we live by exposes the most insidious myth of all, the myth of Art.

The Russian formalist critics have coined a phrase which is an apt description of this author's treatment of his medium: *obnazheniye priyema* (the exposure of the device). The expression describes the process of rendering the reader totally aware of the literary strategies which the author employs. Literature must be seen to be done.

Lautréamont wants the reader to know precisely what he is doing. He attacks the principle that underlies conventional literature: *summa ars artem celare*, whereby the slip into literature is made as unobtrusively as possible. Lautréamont writes as obtrusively as he can.

He begins his exposure of literary technique on the level of syntax. The normal requirement for any literary style is that it should seem 'natural and appropriate'. The conventional stylist seeks to be unobtrusive. We must enjoy his language, but must never be allowed to feel that the language is there simply to be enjoyed. We must feel it to have some element of necessity about it. Above all, if the stylist is to avoid the pitfall of allowing his devices to become over-transparent, he must never lay himself open to the charge that he writes in a manner unmotivated, artificial or contrived.

Style must always be seen to be natural, but one might well ask natural to what? The conception of 'natural style' is well illustrated by the stylistics of Hollywood movies of the fifties and early sixties. The cutting rhythm was always smooth and followed well-established conventions of continuity. There was no unnecessary camera movement. The camera was mounted on a stand as steady as the Rock of Gibraltar. The film was always evenly developed, never over- or under-exposed. Nothing was allowed to interrupt the steady, unobtrusive flow of the picture, just as nothing interrupts the flow of the novel or poem of the nineteenth century. In contrast with Hollywood stylistics, Lautréamont comes across like Godard. He makes his style as

Conclusion

obtrusive and contrived as he can. He wants us to notice it as
something artificial and conventional, rather than mistake it for
reality. To this effect he uses devices such as the following
absurd parody of Latin rhetoric. Mervyn's father has just been
admonishing his children:

> As if that adorable nest of kids could understand rhetoric! He
> spoke, and a wave of his hand directed one of the brothers
> to the paternal library.[3]

He spoke is a direct and ludicrous transposition of the Latin
dixit.

Passages of direct speech point up the unnatural quality of
the style. They are written in such a clumsy, subjunctive-laden
way, that we reflect on the incongruity of such language, and
then perhaps on the no greater incongruity of other renderings
of speech, and finally perhaps on the bizarre nature of speech
itself.

For similar reasons he distorts 'natural' word-order: 'I have
seen them blushing, going pale with shame for their behaviour
on this earth; seldom.'[4] This is distortion for distortion's sake:
one distortion being no greater than another which we accept
simply because we are used to it.

The same attitude underwrites his narrative technique. The
parody of the narrative stock-in-trade of the Gothick novel was
a case in point. Elsewhere he makes us remember that we are
reading a work of fiction. Hence contradictions in terms such
as: 'You have recognised my imaginary hero.'[5] 'Let us recall
the names of those imaginary beings which my pen ... has
drawn from my brain.'[6] In the sixth canto he informs us that he
is creating certain effects:

> I would scarcely know my business as a writer of thrillers,
> were I not to advance the restrictive interrogatives which
> immediately precede what I have just finished.[7]

The lines are followed by the mysterious image of the black
swan with an anvil on its back.

When he indulges in a piece of atmospheric writing, he
makes sure we know as much, writing of 'this spot which my
pen ... has just made mysterious'.[8]

More important than the exposure of his narrative devices

is his treatment of imagery, the mainstay of his rhetoric. We accept the image as the product of a creative imagination which detects secret correspondences, underlying relationships, that are taken from some strange *liber mundi*. This is not so. Imagery is the creation of rhetoric; the arbitrary product of an illusion of resemblance. It is the product of words alone, and has nothing to do with things:

> Generally speaking how strange is that attractive tendency that makes us seek (in order to express them) the similarities and differences that objects as unlike each other as possible, conceal among their natural properties; they are often, on the face of it, least suited to this sort of curiously sympathetic combination, which, on my honour, graciously confers upon the style of the writer who offers himself this personal satisfaction, the impossible and unforgettable expression of an owl, serious to the end of time.[9]

He takes his exposition of imagery further still. Not only does he ask what an image is, he investigates the peculiar nature of French imagery in particular.

His rhetoric has a certain strain that points to a special concern with the patterns of French poetry. Perhaps its favourite syntactic pattern for writing images has a structure that might be expressed as: The A of the B. The expression is a form of predication which relates the two nouns. These tend to name referents that are remote from one another in reality, but that, for the poet, have some secret link. An example would be Hugo's 'la laine des moutons sinistres de la mer' as an image for waves. One can cite countless examples of the construction, notably from the poetry of the period between 1830 and 1930. The construction is so familiar, so natural to the bent of the language, that it is liable to great abuse. It can become a syntactic cliché, a weak link in the French poetic chain.

The perpetual tendency to personify and concretise in this way results in rapid devaluation. So familiar does the construction become that it immediately signals that any words it joins, however remote they may appear, actually belong together. Words are brought into too close a relationship and are bled of their capacity to refer to concrete things. They all move on to an abstract plane where they become pale reflections of qualities—thisness and thatness. The resulting poetry takes on a cerebral, insipid and somewhat pretentious feel, qualities that make up the term that describes the extreme abuse of the device—*préciosité*.

The *précieux* themselves furnish innumerable examples of the deterioriation in concrete meaning that abuse of this construction brings about. A broom becomes the 'instrument of cleanliness' for example. The consequences for modern French poetry are more serious. Abuse of the construction greatly diminishes poetic impact, creating a style that can be utterly insipid and gutless.

Valéry is a great offender in this respect. Consider the line

Tes pas enfants de mon silence

By no means a bad line, it is balanced on a knife-edge. The *enfants de mon silence* render the footsteps so abstract, so much a part of the allegorical account of an inner event—the coming of poetic inspiration—that they virtually cease to have any real presence as footsteps. Compare this with a similar expression, the title of a novel by Brian Aldiss, *Barefoot in the Head*. It is infinitely more concrete and vivid, with none of the abstract insipidity of Valéry's line.

The nature and the abuse of this construction tell us a great deal about the French language as a poetic medium. It is one of the consequences of its evolution, that, largely for phonological reasons, the individual word enjoys a much lower degree of semantic motivation than does its German or even English equivalent. So much have the sound patterns of French changed from the original Latin forms, that their derivation is no longer apparent. The meaning of a French word is not immediately obvious on inspection. Compare the French word for glove, *gant*, with the German *Handschuh*. The words have quite a different semantic feel.

The importance of individual words is even more reduced by the way in which French is spoken. It runs whole series of words into single blocks of sound, where German, or English, accord a greater element of articulatory prominence to individual words. This difference in speech patterns makes for a corresponding difference in the semantic load carried by single words. It makes French words both less meaningful and more abstract—in the sense of more general. Where English or German words have a relatively restricted range of potential meanings, the range of the French word is much broader. The particular meaning intended in a given situation has therefore to be rendered clear by the context in which the word occurs, to a much greater extent than in the Germanic languages. The French word always occurs as part of a cluster, and it is the business of that cluster to determine the particular sense in which the word is intended. French favours words with a wide range of possible meanings, and it relies on a precise and clear context to bring the meanings out. This is why it is described as such an unambiguous language. An excellent example of the way in which French requires one to use more words and be more specific than English is provided by the title to the French version of the Simon and Garfunkel song *Bridge over Troubled Waters*: this becomes *Un pont jeté sur l'eau troublé*. Including the articles this represents an increase from four to seven words. Moreover the French *sur* being less specific than the English *over* requires the addition of *jeté* to render its meaning complete.[10]

This low degree of semantic motivation encourages the proliferation of the A of the B pattern. Abuse of the construction has the effect of placing words in a context in which none of their potential meanings are realised, making for virtual nonsense. Lautréamont seems to have been aware of the danger. He gives us whole series of images that are designed to explode the device. They stretch personification well beyond breaking point, making us think very carefully about the value of the device as such. They share with black humour the use made of incongruity, and participate in the aesthetics of the bad joke. As usual these are bad jokes with a purpose.

The warning that opens *Les Chants* contains an example of excessive personification, violent enough to verge on the ridiculous. It will be recalled that the author warns the reader not to lose 'his rough and wild path across the desolate marshes of these sombre, poison-ridden pages'.[11] This intricate expression which, in the original, has the unfortunate assonance of *marécages* and *pages,* makes the image incongruous enough. Moreover the marshes are given too great a measure of physical reality to blend happily with the pages. The expression places a lot of strain on the A of the B rhetorical pattern.

The author grows closer to a parody of *précieux* rhetoric when he writes of the hermaphrodite who draws away 'on the wings of his watchful modesty and disappears into the forest'.[12] The personification is too strange to be entirely innocent. As much is true of the following blend of abstract and concrete: 'Once again he withdraws into the immobility of his egoism like a tortoise into his shell.'[13] This looks like a booby-trap. It is too strange to take at face value. Just how strange the author can get is illustrated by the following shameless parody of the *précieux*: 'The octopus of weakness of character, the shark of personal abjection, the boa of absent morality and the monstrous snail of idiocy.'[14] The trap is finally sprung when he takes the language of personification apart once and for all, writing that 'tortures ... passed before my brow roaring like flayed elephants, brushing my charred hair with their wings of fire'.[15] As usual Lautréamont has the last word.

We come now to the most important relationship in the book; that between author and reader. The author has made it clear throughout that he is performing for his reader's benefit, not for his own. Ducasse, once an unhappy schoolboy, discovered the shortcomings of official education, and, by extension, official culture, the hard way. In turn he is going to do his utmost to teach his readers, but to teach them in such a way that they are broadened, not narrowed, by the process.

In order that the reader get as much as he can from his work, Lautréamont begins each canto with a discussion of his writing. It often takes the form of a set of instructions. In the first canto he warns us to tackle the writing logically, to keep our mental cool. He also warns us that the work may appeal to our secret selves. The second canto introduces the paradigm of injunctions designed to reveal the nature of the so-called creative process. This consists of the inscription of words on a sheet of paper. There is nothing else. It to begins: 'I take up the pen that will construct the second canto . . .'[16] It is not a coincidence that it continues with a parody of Musset's *Nuit de Mai*—romanticism's most eloquent homage to the creative fallacy.

The third canto reminds us that we are reading fiction, it

refers to 'imaginary beings of angelic nature that my pen drew from my brain in the second canto'.[17]

The fifth canto contains the crucial passage begging the reader not to be angry should the author's prose fail to please him. It goes on to warn him against partial truth and ends with the description of the flock of starlings.

Elsewhere he reminds us that we are reading the printed word, not some stone tablet found on a mountain-top. He checks a digression 'in order to get no further away from this sheet of paper'.[18] On another occasion he is having a bad time, but this does not prevent him from carrying on with the mechanical business of writing: 'I shall still have the strength to raise the pen.'[19] He sometimes feels the whole business of scratching signs on paper to be utterly absurd. He takes great care that we should remain aware of the purely physical circumstances of writing, lest we suppose for a moment that the words are signs referring to some mysterious area of meaning beyond themselves and out of this world: 'I find it stupid that ... I must place beside me an open inkwell and a few sheets of *papier non mâché.*'[20]

The author uses such phrases to drive his message home. We live in a culture that surrounds us with signs, we are haunted by them. From learned journals to billboards our environment is sign-saturated. It is the business of signs to trick us into looking through and beyond the two-dimensional space in which they have their being, to send us through the billboard into one or another of the infinity of parallel dream-worlds that are generated by each brand and product; just as the learned journal seeks to send us into a stratosphere in which arguments and concepts caper in elegant patterns to some scholar's tune.

The media all seek to take us through their particular looking-glass, and persuade us that the world that we find on the other side is our, not their, reality—that they tell it like it is.

Lautréamont reminds us that they do nothing of the sort. With his references to pen, paper and ink, he reminds us that the so-called looking-glass is a flat opaque surface; a mere dream-machine designed to put into our heads pictures that tempt us to treat them as if they were real.

The clarity with which Lautréamont expresses these ideas is

also his own undoing. He is too aware of the nature of the literary processes to be taken in by his own illusions. Finally, and paradoxically, he knows himself to be cut off from his hero— the reader. For it is the reader who is the real object of his sexual desire. In true Socratic or Gidean manner, he has been attempting both his education and his seduction. Unfortunately the loved one must for ever remain on the wrong side of his words. The paper is too resilient a looking-glass to permit Ducasse to pass through it. He is obliged to remain alone with the unreal creations of his dream world:

> Why can I not see the face of my reader through these seraphic pages. If he has not passed the age of puberty let him approach. Hold me against you and do not fear to hurt me . . . More! I feel it is useless to insist; the opacity of this sheet of paper, remarkable in more ways than one, is the most formidable of obstacles.[21]

It is in the interests of the reader's education, an education that must, also, be free of sentiment, that Ducasse has been executing these extraordinary antics. By no means lacking in ambition, he seeks to unfold the whole basis of our place in the world, to sketch out the range of human possibility. He tries to make us see that our experience of the world is formed by a dualistic thought process. His book is not about good and evil, or even about prose and poetry, but about dualism. The pairings he examines, and all possible pairings, derive from a mental and linguistic structure that we can neither slough off nor transcend, but which we can, perhaps, learn to live with.

It is vitally important that we should do so, should get wise to ourselves. In science-fiction's innumerable political allegories of a totalitarian future, there is one common element; the majority of the population are not even aware that they are being manipulated. In other words they are so oblivious of their particular cultural prison, that they sit happily in cells so tiny that they would not use them as hen-coops.

The greater our awareness of how we think, and of the way in which culture does our thinking for us, the less likely we shall be to mistake the plastic daydream for the real thing. The more we appreciate that our view of reality is determined by the pattern of our thinking, the clearer our picture of that reality will become.

A quick practical illustration of this point can be seen in the American foreign policy of the Dulles era. So haunted was it by a sense of dualism whereby you were either 'for us or against us' that it invented the domino theory. It took twenty years for the USA to discover the existence of a third world—a whole range of cultures that did not fit into its crude political calculus. By then it was too late to do anything but destroy the whole of Vietnam, in order to avoid the loss of face that would have resulted had the descendants of Colonel Custer been obliged to make a stand at a second Dien Bien Phu. The failure to appraise the situation was not a simple question of failing to notice the existence of a third world. It was a case of, literally and in the full sense of the term, being unable to perceive it. A mental grid that placed all 'slits, ginks and gooks' in a single category was simply too coarse to be able to handle the third world concept.

Lautréamont writes to help us to refine our mental grid. He tries to make us think of the relationship between *Les Chants* and *Poésies* not in terms of good and evil, law and anarchy, pleasure principle and reality principle, because we live in a dualistic world in which each one signifies the other anyway. It is law that makes transgression possible, and crime that creates the law. The author has used his text to build a verbal model designed to expose those dualisms for what they are: mere conventions of thought and perception, the basis of all forms of communication and social relationship. He tries, in a paraphrase of Marcelin Pleynet, to describe the 'place in which you can hear and be heard' : to describe the context of communication, the circumstances that make all conceivable forms of code conceivable.

Lautréamont takes on the impossible task of being anthropologist to the human race, of describing man and his place in the world in terms which are not circular. Such an endeavour must lead to total silence, and perhaps silence itself is a human quality. Lautréamont is looking for a germ-free language with which to talk to man without any humanistic aforethought. He wants a perfect metalanguage.[22] But there is no such thing, since all human symbol-systems are humanity-bound. Yet he has gone a long way towards the creation of a 'new science', an instrument both technical and poetic, that will serve as a means of demystification and, even more important, of demythification, on all levels of human experience : science, technology, philosophy, literature, ethics and religion. Such a language is sterilised but not sterile. The awareness of this language remains with us as a possibility. It is that possibility, with its utterly moral and educational purpose, that makes the final impression of *Les Chants*, despite its sexual violence, its obscenity, its blasphemy, its bitter and often puerile savagery, one of a unique and untarnished innocence.

Notes

All references to Lautréamont's *Oeuvres* are to *Oeuvres Complètes*, published by Editions de la Pléiade (Paris 1970).

Introduction to Nightmare
1. Quoted by E. Cassirer, *Language and Myth* (New York 1946), p. 9.
2. Il est temps de serrer les freins à mon inspiration, et de m'arrêter, un instant, en route, comme quand on regarde le vagin d'une femme. Lautréamont, *Oeuvres*, p. 129.
3. Plût au ciel que le lecteur, enhardi et devenu momentanément féroce comme ce qu'il lit, trouve, sans se désorienter, son chemin abrupt et sauvage, à travers les marécages désolés de ces pages sombres et pleines de poison; car, à moins qu'il n'apporte dans sa lecture une logique rigoureuse et une tension d'esprit égale au moins à sa défiance, les émanations mortelles de ce livre imbiberont son âme comme l'eau le sucre. *op. cit.*, p. 45.

One   In Place of a Biography
1. *Oeuvres*, p. 268.
2. H. Berlioz, *Mémoires* (Paris 1969 ed.), Vol. I, p. 121.
3. *op. cit.*, p. 285.

Two   The Life of Isidore Ducasse
1. *Oeuvres*, p. 296.
2. *loc. cit.*
3. *op. cit.*, p. 297.
4. E. Peyrouzet, *Vie de Lautréamont* (Paris 1970).
5. *Oeuvres*, pp. 1024–7.
6. J. Henry. *Culture Against Man* (London 1966), p. 287.
7. Henry, p. 286.
8. Henry, pp. 287–8.
9. Henry, p. 305.
10. Quand un élève interne, dans un lycée, est gouverné, pendant des années, qui sont des siècles, du matin jusqu'au soir et du soir jusqu'au lendemain, par un paria de la civilisation, qui a constamment les yeux sur lui, il sent les flots tumultueux d'une haine vivace, monter, comme une épaisse fumée, à son cerveau, qui lui paraît près d'éclater. Depuis le moment où on l'a jeté dans la prison, jusqu'à celui, qui s'approche, où il en sortira, une fièvre intense lui jaunit la face, rapproche ses sourcils, et lui creuse les yeux. *Oeuvres*, pp. 70–1.

Three   Le Comte de Lautréamont and the Media I
1. Le plagiat est nécessaire. Le progrès l'implique. Il serre de près la phrase d'un auteur, se sert de ses expressions, efface une idée fausse, la remplace par l'idée juste. *Oeuvres*, p. 281.

169

2. Je crois avoir enfin trouvé, après quelques tâtonnements, ma formule définitive. C'est la meilleure: puisque c'est le roman! *op. cit.*, p. 221.

Four Le Comte de Lautréamont and the Media II

1. *Mas Media and Mass Man*, ed. A. Casty (London 1968), p. 232.

2. M'emparant d'un style que quelques-uns trouveront naïf (quand il est si profond), je le ferai servir à interpréter des idées qui, malheureusement, ne paraîtront peut-être pas grandioses! *Ouevres*, p. 223.

3. Il va de contrée en contrée, abhorré partout. Les uns disent qu'il est accablé d'une espèce de folie originelle, depuis son enfance. D'autres croient savoir qu'il est d'une cruauté extrême et instinctive, dont il a honte lui-même, et que ses parents en sont morts de douleur.

Il y en a qui prétendent qu'on l'a flétri d'un surnom dans sa jeunesse; qu'il en est resté inconsolable le reste de son existence, parce que sa dignité blessée voyait là une preuve flagrante de la méchanceté des hommes, qui se montre aux premières années, pour augmenter ensuite. Ce surnom était *le vampire!* . . . *op. cit.*, pp. 65–6.

4. Il savait que la police, ce bouclier de la civilisation, le recherchait avec persévérance, depuis nombre d'années, et qu'une véritable armée d'agents et de'espions était continuellement à ses trousses. San, cependant, parvenir à le rencontrer. Tant son habileté renversante déroutait, avec un suprême chic, les ruses les plus indiscutables au point de vue de leur succès, et l'ordonnance de la plus savante méditation. Il avait une faculté spéciale pour prendre des formes méconnaissables aux yeux exercés. Déguisements supérieurs, si je parle en artiste! . . . Par ce point, il touchait presque au génie. N'avez-vous pas remarqué la gracilité d'un joli grillon, aux mouvements alertes, dans les égouts de Paris? . . . Maldoror! . . . Aujourd'hui il est à Madrid; demain il sera à Saint-Pétersbourg; hier il se trouvait à Pékin. Ce bandit est, peut-être, à sept cents lieues de ce pays; peut-être, il est à quelques pas de vous. *op. cit.*, p. 222.

5. Comment le pont du Carrousel put-il garder la constance de sa neutralité, lorsqu'il entendit les cris déchirants que semblait pousser le sac! *op. cit.*, p. 223.

6. Dirigez-vous du côté où se trouve le lac des cygnes; et, je vous dirai plus tard pourquoi il s'en trouve un de complètement noir parmi la troupe, et dont le corps, supportant une enclume, surmontée du cadavre en putréfaction d'un crabe tourteau, inspire à bon droit de la méfiance à ses autres aquatiques camarades. *op. cit.*, pp. 229–30.

7. La queue de poisson ne volera que pendant trois jours, c'est vrai; mais, hélas! la poutre n'en sera pas moins brûlée; et une balle cylindroconique percera la peau du rhinocéros, malgré la fille de neige et le mendiant! C'est que le fou couronné aura dit la vérité sur le fidélité des quatorze poignards. *op. cit.*, pp. 234–5.

8. Quoted by Marshall McLuhan, *The Gutenberg Galaxy* (London 1962), pp. 36–8.

Five Maldoror

1. Dans la crainte qu'il ne devînt plus tard comme les autres hommes, j'avais d'abord résolu de le tuer à coups de couteau, lorsqu'il aurait dépassé l'âge d'innocence. Mais, j'ai réfléchi, et j'ai abandonné sagement ma résolution à temps. Il ne se doute pas que sa vie a été en péril pendant un quart d'heure. Tout était prêt, et le couteau avait été acheté. Ce stylet était mignon, car j'aime la grâce et l'élégance jusque dans les appareils de la mort; mais il

était long et pointu. Une seule blessure au cou, en perçant avec soin une des artères carotides, et je crois que ç'aurait suffi. *Oeuvres*, p. 84.

2. Jusqu'a ce que j'aperçusse un trône, formé d'excréments humains et d'or, sur lequel trônait, avec un orgueil idiot, le corps recouvert d'un linceul fait avec des draps non lavés d'hôpital, celui qui s'intitule lui-même le Créateur! Il tenait à la main le tronc pourri d'un homme mort, et le portait, alternativement, des yeux au nez et du nez à la bouche; une fois à la bouche, on divine ce qu'il en faisait. Ses pieds plongeaient dans une vaste mare de sang en ébullition, à la surface duquel s'élevaient tout à coup, comme des ténias à travers le contenu d'un pot de chambre, deux ou trois têtes prudentes, et qui s'abaissaient aussitôt, avec la rapidité de la flèche: un coup de pied, bien appliqué sur l'os du nez, était la récompense connue de la révolte au règlement, occasionnée par le besoin de respirer un autre milieu; car, enfin, ces hommes n'étaient pas des poissons! Amphibies tout au plus, ils nageaient entre deux eaux dans ce liquide immonde! . . . jusqu'à ce que, n'ayant plus rien dans la main, le Créateur, avec les deux premières griffes du pied, saisît un autre plongeur par le cou, comme dans une tenaille, et le soulevât en l'air, en dehors de la vase rougeâtre, sauce exquise! Pour celui-là, il faisait comme pour l'autre. Il lui dévorait d'abord la tête, les jambes et les bras, et en dernier lieu le tronc, jusqu'à ce qu'il ne restât plus rien; car, il croquait les os. Ainsi de suite, durant les autres heures de son éternité. Quelquefois il s'écriait: 'Je vous ai créés; donc j'ai le droit de faire de vous ce que je veux. Vous ne m'avez rien fait, je ne dis pas le contraire. Je vous fais souffrir, et c'est pour mon plaisir.' Et il reprenait son repas cruel, en remuant sa mâchoire inférieure, laquelle remuait sa barbe pleine de cervelle. O lecteur, ce dernier détail ne te fait-il pas venir l'eau à la bouche? N'en mange pas qui veut d'une pareille cervelle, si bonne, toute fraîche, et qui vient d'être pêchée il n'y a qu'un quart d'heure dans le lac aux *poissons*. Les membres paralysés, et la gorge muette, je contemplai quelque temps ce spectacle. Trois fois, je faillis tomber à la renverse, comme un homme qui subit une émotion trop forte; trois fois, je parvins à me remettre sur les pieds. Pas une fibre de mon corps ne restait immobile; et je tremblais, comme tremble la lave intérieure d'un volcan. A la fin, ma poitrine oppressée, ne pouvant chasser avec assez de vitesse l'air qui donne la vie, les lèvres de ma bouche s'entrouvrirent, et je poussai un cri . . . un cri si déchirant . . . que je l'entendis! Les entraves de mon oreille se délièrent d'une manière brusque, le tympan craqua sous le choc de cette masse d'air sonore repoussée loin de moi avec énergie, et il se passa un phénomène nouveau dans l'organe condamné par la nature. Je venais d'entendre un son! Un cinquième sens se révélait en moi! *op cit.*, pp. 97–9.

3. L'Eternel a créé le monde tel qu'il est; il montrerait beaucoup de sagesse si, pendant le temps strictement nécessaire pour briser d'un coup de marteau la tête d'une femme, il oubliait sa majesté sidérale, afin de nous révéler les mystères au milieu desquels notre existence étouffe, comme un poisson au fond d'une barque. *op. cit.*, p. 83.

4. Ainsi donc, Maldoro, tu as vaincu l'*Espérance*! Désormais, le désespoir se nourrira de ta substance la plus pure! Désormais, tu rentres, à pas délibérés, dans la carrière du mal! *op. cit.*, p. 143.

5. Oh! si au lieu d'être un enfer, l'univers n'avait été qu'un céleste anus immense, regardez le geste que je fais du côté de mon bas-ventre; oui, j'aurais enfoncé ma verge, à travers son sphincter sanglant, fracassant, par mes mouvements impétueux, les propres parois de son bassin! Le malheur

n'aurait pas alors soufflé, sur mes yeux aveuglés . . . j'aurais découvert l'endroit souterrain où gît la vérité endormie. *op. cit.*, p. 203.

6. En effet, j'arrache le masque à sa figure traîtresse et pleine de boue, et je fais tomber un à un . . . les mensonges sublimes avec lesquels il se trompe lui-même. *op cit.*, p. 79.

7. *op. cit.*, p. 77.

8. Nietzsche, *Thus Spake Zarathustra* (London 1961 ed.), p. 142.

9. C'est pourquoi, le héros que je mets en scène s'est attiré une haine irréconciliable, en attaquant l'humanité, qui se croyait invulnérable. *op. cit.*, p. 80.

10. [Le poète] ne prétend pas que ses cavatines soient une chose inconnue; au contraire, il se loue de ce que les pensées hautaines et méchantes de son héros soient dans tous les hommes. *op. cit.*, p. 47.

11. Il s'aperçut ensuite qu'il était né méchant : fatalité extraordinaire! . . . Humains, avez-vous entendu? il ose le redire avec cette plume qui tremble! *op. cit.*, pp. 46–7.

12. peindre les délices de la cruauté! Délices non passagères, artificielles; . . . parce qu'on est cruel, ne peut-on pas avoir de génie? *op. cit.*, p. 47.

13. qu'il n'était composé que de bien et d'une quantité minime de mal. Brusquement je lui appris, en découvrant au plein jour son coeur et ses trames, qu'au contraire, il n'est composé que de mal, et d'une quantité minime de bien que les législateurs ont de la peine à ne pas laisser évaporer. *op. cit.*, p. 79.

14. l'homme dit hypocritement oui et pense non. C'est pour cela que les marcassins de l'humanité ont tant de confiance les uns dans les autres et ne sont pas égoïstes. Il reste à la psychologie beaucoup de progrès à faire. *op. cit.*, p. 59.

15. Lecteur, c'est peut-être la haine que tu veux que j'invoque dans le commencement de cet ouvrage! Qui te dit que tu n'en renifleras pas, baigné dans d'innombrables voluptés, tant que tu voudras, avec tes narines orgueilleuses, larges et maigres, en te renversant de ventre, pareil à un requin, dans l'air beau et noir, comme si tu comprenais l'importance de cet acte et l'importance non moindre de ton appétit légitime, lentement et majestueusement, les rouges émanations? Je t'assure, elles réjouiront les deux trous informes de ton museau hideux, ô monstre. *op. cit.*, p. 46.

16. *The Republic* (London 1955 ed.), p. 191.

17. Tu vois que, lorsqu'on veut devenir célèbre, il faut se plonger avec grâce dans des fleuves de sang, alimentés par de la chair à canon. *op. cit.*, p. 92.

Six   Black Humour and the Absurd

1. Ils ne pouvaient échapper! Par surcroît de précaution, j'avais été chercher mon fusil à deux coups, afin que, si quelque naufragé était tenté d'aborder les rochers à la nage, pour échapper à une mort imminente, une balle sur l'épaule lui fracassât le bras, et l'empêchât d'accomplir son dessein. Au moment le plus furieux de la tempête, je vis, surnageant sur les eaux, avec des efforts désespérés, une tête énergique, aux cheveux hérissés. Il avalait des litres d'eau, et s'enfonçait dans l'abîme, ballotté comme un liège. Mais, bientôt, il apparaissait de nouveau, les cheveux ruisselants; et, fixant l'oeil sur le rivage, il semblait défier la mort. Il était admirable de sang-froid. Une large blessure sanglante, occasionnée par quelque pointe d'écueil caché, balafrait son visage intrépide et noble. Il ne devait pas avoir plus de seize ans; car, à peine, à travers les éclairs qui illuminaient la nuit, le duvet de la

pêche s'apercevait sur sa lèvre. Et, maintenant, il n'était plus qu'à deux cents mètres de la falaise; et je le dévisageais facilement. Quel courage! Quel esprit indomptable! Comme la fixité de sa tête semblait narguer le destin, tout en fendant avec vigueur l'onde, dont les sillons s'ouvraient difficilement devant lui! . . . Je l'avais décidé d'avance. Je me devais à moi-même de tenir ma promesse: l'heure dernière avait sonné pour tous, aucun ne devait en échapper. Voilà ma résolution; rien ne la changerait . . . Un son sec s'entendit, et la tête aussitôt s'enfonça, pour ne plus reparaître. Je ne pris à ce meurtre autant de plaisir qu'on pourrait le croire; et, c'était, précisément, parce que j'étais rassasié de toujours tuer, que je le faisais dorénavant par simple habitude, dont on ne peut se passer, mais, qui ne procure qu'une jouissance légère. *Oeuvres,* pp. 119–20.

2. A. Artaud, 'Le Théâtre et son Double'. In *Oeuvres Complètes* (1964 ed.), Vol. IV, p. 52 (author's translation).

3. *Ibid.,* p. 121.

4. On doit laisser pousser ses ongles pendant quinze jours. Oh! comme il est doux d'arracher brutalement de son lit un enfant qui n'a rien encore sur la lèvre supérieure, et, avec les yeux très ouverts, de faire semblant de passer suavement la main sur son front, en inclinant en arrière ses beaux cheveux! Puis, tout à coup, au moment où il s'y attend le moins, d'enfoncer les ongles longs dans sa poitrine molle, de façon qu'il ne meure pas; car, s'il mourait, on n'aurait pas plus tard l'aspect de ses misères. Ensuite, on boit le sang en léchant les blessures; et, pendant ce temps, qui devrait durer autant que l'éternité dure, l'enfant pleure. Rien n'est si bon que son sang, extrait comme je viens de le dire, et tout chaud encore, si ce ne sont ses larmes, amères comme le sel . . . Bande-lui les yeux, pendant que tu déchireras ses chairs palpitantes; et, après avoir entendu de longues heures ses cris sublimes . . . tu te précipiteras de la chambre voisine, et tu feras semblant d'arriver à son secours. Tu lui délieras les mains, aux nerfs et aux veines gonflées, tu rendras la vue à ses yeux égarés, en te remettant à lécher ses larmes et son sang. Comme alors le repentir est vrai! L'étincelle divine qui est en nous, et paraît si rarement, se montre; trop tard! *Oeuvres,* pp. 49–50.

5. Je pourrais, en prenant ta tête entre mes mains, d'un air caressant et doux, enfoncer mes doigts avides dans les lobes de ton cerveau innocent, pour en extraire, le sourire aux lèvres, une graisse efficace qui lave mes yeux, endoloris par l'insomnie éternelle de la vie. Je pourrais, cousant tes paupières avec une aiguille, te priver du spectacle de l'univers, et te mettre dans l'impossibilité de trouver ton chemin; ce n'est pas moi qui te servirai de guide. *op. cit.,* p. 89.

6. Maldoror passait avec son bouledogue; il voit une jeune fille qui dort à l'ombre d'un platane, et il la prit d'abord pour une rose . . . Il se déshabille rapidement, comme un homme qui sait ce qu'il va faire. Nu comme une pierre, il s'est jeté sur le corps de la jeune fille, et lui a levé la robe pour commettre un attentat à la pudeur . . . à la clarté du soleil! Il ne se gênera pas, allez! . . . N'insistons pas sur cette action impure. L'esprit mécontent, il se rhabille avec précipitation, jette un regard de prudence sur la route poudreuse, où personne ne chemine, et ordonne au bouledogue d'étrangler avec le mouvement de ses mâchoires, la jeune fille ensanglantée. Il indique au chien de la montagne la place où respire et hurle la victime souffrante, et se retire à l'écart, pour ne pas être témoin de la rentrée des dents pointues dans les veines roses. L'accomplissement de cet ordre put paraître sévère au bouledogue. Il crut qu'on lui demanda ce qui avait été déjà fait, et se contenta, ce loup, au mufle monstrueux, de violer à son tour la virginité

de cette enfant délicate. De son ventre déchiré, le sang coule de nouveau le long de ses jambes, à travers la prairie. Ses gémissements se joignent au pleurs de l'animal. La jeune fille lui présente la croix d'or qui ornait son cou, afin qu'il l'épargne; elle n'avait pas osé la présenter aux yeux farouches de celui qui, d'abord, avait eu la pensée de profiter de la faiblesse de son âge. Mais le chien n'ignorait pas que, s'il désobéissait à son maître, un couteau lancé de dessous une manche, ouvrirait brusquement ses entrailles, sans crier gare. Maldoror (comme ce nom répugne à prononcer!) entendait les agonies de la douleur, et s'étonnait que la victime eût la vie si dure, pour ne pas être encore morte. Il s'approche de l'autel sacrificatoire, et voit la conduite de son bouledogue, livré à de bas penchants, et qui élevait sa tête au-dessus de la jeune fille, comme un naufragé élève la sienne, au, dessus des vagues en courroux. Il lui donne un coup de pied et lui fend un œil. Le bouledogue, en colère, s'enfuit dans la campagne, entraînant apres lui, pendant un espace de route qui est toujours trop long, pour si court qu'il fût, le corps de la jeune fille suspendue, qui n'a été dégagé que grâce aux mouvements saccadés de la fuite; mais, il craint d'attaquer son maître, qui ne le reverra plus. Celui-ci tire de sa poche un canif américain, composé de dix à douze lames qui servent à divers usages. Il ouvre les pattes anguleuses de cet hydre d'acier; et, muni d'un pareil scalpel, voyant que le gazon n'avait pas encore disparu sous la couleur de tant de sang versé, s'apprête, sans pâlir, à fouiller courageusement le vagin de la malheureuse enfant. De ce trou élargi, il retire successivement les organes intérieurs; les boyaux, les poumons, le foie, et enfin le coeur lui-même sont arrachés de leurs fondements et entraînés à la lumière du jour, par l'ouverture épouvantable. Le sacrificateur s'aperçoit que la jeune fille, poulet vidé, est morte depuis longtemps. *op. cit.*, pp. 139–40.

7. Oh! . . . voyez! . . . voyez donc! la joue blanche et rose est devenue noire, comme un charbon! Elle exhale des miasmes putrides. C'est la gangrène; il n'est plus permis d'en douter. *op. cit.*, p. 111.

8. Malheur au voyageur attardé! Les amis des cimetières se jetteront sur lui, le déchireront, le mangeront, avec leur bouche d'où tombe du sang; car, ils n'ont pas les dents gâtées. *op. cit.*, p. 54.

9. Sans doute, le corps est resté plaqué sur la muraille, comme une poire mûre, et n'est pas tombé à terre; mais, les chiens savent accomplir des bonds élevés, si l'on n'y prend garde. *op. cit.*, p. 90.

10. tu [as] cru, en outre, convenable à ta majesté, après un mûr examen, de faire sortir de mon front une coupe de sang! *op. cit.*, p. 81.

11. J'ai vu, pendant toute ma vie, sans en excepter un seul, les hommes, aux épaules étroites, faire des actes stupides et nombreux, abrutir leurs semblables, et pervertir les âmes par tous les moyens. Ils appellent les motifs de leur actions: la gloire. En voyant ces spectacles, j'ai voulu rire comme les autres; mais, cela, étrange imitation, était impossible. J'ai pris un canif dont la lame avait un tranchant acéré, et me suis fendu les chairs aux endroits où se réunissent les lèvres. Un instant je crus mon but atteint. Je regardai dans un miroir cette bouche meurtrie par ma propre volonté! C'était une erreur! Le sang qui coulait avec abondance des deux blessures empêchait d'ailleurs de distinguer si c'était là vraiment le rire des autres. Mais, après quelques instants de comparaison, je vis bien que mon rire ne ressemblait pas à celui des humains, c'est-à-dire que je ne riais pas. *op. cit.*, pp. 47–8.

12. Chacun se dit qu'une fois dans l'eau, il ne pourra plus respirer; car, d'aussi loin qu'il fait revenir sa mémoire, il ne se reconnaît aucun poisson

pour ancêtre; mais, il s'exhorte à retenir son souffle le plus longtemps possible, afin de prolonger sa vie de deux ou trois secondes, *op. cit.*, p. 118.

13. Pardon, il me semblait que mes cheveux s'étaient dressés sur ma tête; mais, ce n'est rien, car, avec ma main, je suis parvenu facilement à les remettre dans leur première position. *op. cit.*, p. 47.

14. l'apparence sérieuse de ce qui n'est en somme que grotesque. *op. cit.*, p. 160.

15. Souvent, il m'arrivera d'énoncer, avec solennité, les propositions les plus bouffonnes. *op. cit.*, p. 77.

16. Adieu donc; n'espère plus retrouver le crapaud sur ton passage. Tu as été la cause de ma mort. Moi, je pars pour l'éternité, afin d'implorer ton pardon! *op. cit.*, p. 77.

17. Ni moi, ni les quatre pattes-nageoires de l'ours marin de l'océan Boréal, n'avons pu trouver le problème de la vie. *op. cit.*, p. 75.

18. L'éléphant se laisse caresser. Le pou, non. *op. cit.*, p. 101.

19. cependant, il est permis à chacun de tuer des mouches et même des rhinocéros. *op. cit.*, p. 160.

20. Le coq ne sort pas de sa nature . . . Apprenez-leur à lire, ils se révoltent. Ce n'est pas un perroquet. *op. cit.*, p. 162.

21. j'ai vu une figue manger un âne! Et, cependant, je n'ai pas ri. *op. cit.*, p. 161.

Seven The Ideology of the Absurd
1. Artaud, *op. cit.*, p. 139.
2. Jarry, *Oeuvres Complètes* (Monaco 1948), Vol. V, p. 257.
3. J. G. Ballard, 'The Coming of the Unconscious' in *The Overloaded Man* (London, Panther ed. 1967), p. 144.

Eight Anatomy of a Nightmare
1. Il est minuit; on ne voit plus un seul omnibus de la Bastille à la Madeleine. Je me trompe; en voilà un qui apparaît subitement, comme s'il sortait de dessous terre. Les quelques passants attardés le regardent attentivement; car, il paraît ne ressembler à aucun autre. Sont assis, à l'impériale, des hommes qui ont l'œil immobile, comme celui d'un poisson mort. Ils sont pressés les uns contre les autres, et paraissent avoir perdu la vie; au reste, le nombre réglementaire n'est pas dépassé. Lorsque le cocher donne un coup de fouet à ses chevaux, on dirait que c'est le fouet qui fait remuer son bras, et non son bras le fouet. Que doit être cet assemblage d'êtres bizarres et muets? Sont-ce des habitants de la lune? Il y a des moments où on serait tenté de le croire; mais, ils ressemblent plutôt à des cadavres. L'omnibus, pressé d'arriver à la dernière station, dévore l'espace, et fait craquer le pavé . . . Il s'enfuit! . . . Mais, une masse informe le poursuit avec acharnement, sur ses traces, au milieu de la poussière. 'Arrêtez, je vous en supplie; arrêtez . . . mes jambes sont gonflées d'avoir marché pendant la journée . . . je n'ai pas mangé depuis hier . . . mes parents m'ont abandonné . . . je ne sais plus que faire . . . je suis résolu de retourner chez moi, et j'y serais vite arrivé, si vous m'accordiez une place . . . je suis un petit enfant de huit ans, et j'ai confiance en vous . . .' Il s'enfuit! . . . Il s'enfuit! . . . Mais, une masse informe le poursuit avec acharnement, sur ses traces, au milieu de la poussière. Un de ces hommes, à l'œil froid, donne un coup de coude à son voisin, et paraît lui exprimer son mécontentement de ces gémissements, au timbre argentin, qui parviennent jusqu'à son oreille. L'autre baisse la tête d'une manière imperceptible, en forme d'acquiescement,

et se replonge ensuite dans l'immobilité de son égoïsme, comme une tortue dans sa carapace. *Oeuvres*, pp. 85–6.

2. Il y a des heures dans la vie où l'homme, à la chevelure pouilleuse, jette, l'oeil fixe, des regards fauves sur les membranes vertes de l'espace; car, il lui semble entendre, devant lui, les ironiques huées d'un fantôme. Il chancelle et courbe le tête: ce qu'il a entendu, c'est la voix de la conscience. Alors, il s'élance de la maison, avec la vitesse d'un fou . . . Mais, le fantôme jaune ne le perd pas de vue, et le poursuit avec une égale vitesse. Quelquefois, dans une nuit d'orage, pendant que des légions de poulpes ailés, ressemblant de loin à des corbeaux, planent au-dessus des nuages, en se dirigeant d'une rame raide vers les cités des humains, avec la mission de les avertir de changer de conduite, le caillou, à l'œil sombre, voit deux êtres passer à la lueur de l'éclair, l'un derrière l'autre; et, essuyant une furtive larme de compassion, qui coule de sa paupière glacée, il s'écrie: 'Certes, il le mérite; et ce n'est que justice!' Après avoir dit cela, il se replace dans son attitude farouche, et continue de regarder, avec un tremblement nerveux, la chasse à l'homme, et les grandes lèvres du vagin d'ombre, d'où découlent, sans cesse, comme un fleuve, d'immenses spermatozoïdes ténébreux qui prennent leur essor dans l'éther lugubre, en cachant, avec le vaste déploiement de leurs ailes de chauve-souris, la nature entière, et les légions solitaires de poulpes, devenues mornes à l'aspect de ces fulgurations sourdes et inexprimables. *op. cit.*, p. 125.

3. un ver luisant, grand comme une maison. *op. cit.*, p. 51.

4. animal articulé n'était pas de beaucoup plus grand qu'une vache! *op. cit.*, p. 190.

5. Il existe un insecte que les hommes nourrissent à leurs frais. Ils ne lui doivent rien; mais, ils le craignent. Celui-ci, qui n'aime pas le vin, mais qui préfère le sang, si on ne satisfait pas à ses besoins légitimes, serait capable, par un pouvoir occulte, de devenir aussi gros qu'un éléphant, d'écraser les hommes comme des épis. Aussi faut-il voir comme on le respecte, comme on l'entoure d'une vénération canine, comme on le place en haute estime au-dessus des animaux de la création. On lui donne la tête pour trône, et lui, accroche ses griffes à la racine des cheveux, avec dignité. Plus tard, lorsqu'il est gras et qu'il entre dans un âge avancé, en imitant la coutume d'un peuple ancien, on le tue, afin de ne pas lui faire sentir les atteintes de la vieillesse. On lui fait des funérailles grandioses, comme à un héros, et la bière, qui le conduit directement vers le couvercle de la tombe, est portée, sur les épaules, par les principaux citoyens. Sur la terre humide que le fossoyeur remue avec sa pelle sagace, on combine des phrases multicolores sur l'immortalité de l'âme, sur le néant de la vie, sur la volonté inexplicable de la Providence, et le marbre se referme, à jamais, sur cette existence, laborieusement remplie, qui n'est plus qu'un cadavre. La foule se disperse et la nuit ne tarde pas à couvrir de ses ombres les murailles du cimetière.

Mais, consolez-vous, humains, de sa perte douloureuse. Voici sa famille innombrable, qui s'avance, et dont il vous a libéralement gratifié, afin que votre désespoir fût moins amer, et comme adouci par la présence agréable de ces avortons horgneux, qui deviendront plus tard de magnifiques poux, ornés d'une beauté remarquable, monstres à allure de sage. Il a couvé plusieurs douzaines d'oeufs chéris, avec son aile maternelle, sur vos cheveux desséchés par la succion acharnée de ces étrangers redoutables. La période est promptement venue, où les œufs ont éclaté. Ne craignez rien, ils ne tarderont pas à grandir, ces adolescents philosophes, à travers cette

vie éphémère. Ils grandiront tellement, qu'ils vous le feront sentir, avec leurs griffes et leurs suçoirs.

Vous ne savez pas, vous autres, pourquoi ils ne dévorent pas les os de votre tête, et qu'ils se contentent d'extraire, avec leur pompe, la quintessence de votre sang. Attendez un instant, je vais vous le dire: c'est parce qu'ils n'en ont pas la force. Soyez certains que, si leur mâchoire était conforme à la mesure de leurs vœux infinis, la cervelle, la rétine des yeux, la colonne vertébrale, tout votre corps y passerait. Comme une goutte d'eau. Malheur au cachalot qui se battrait contre un pou. Il serait dévoré en un clin d'œil, malgré sa taille. Il ne resterait pas la queue pour aller annoncer la nouvelle. L'éléphant se laisse caresser. Le pou, non. Je ne vous conseille pas de tenter cet essai périlleux. Gare à vous, si votre main est poilue, ou que seulement elle soit composée d'os et de chair. C'en est fait de vos doigts. *op. cit.*, pp. 100–1.

6. mon visage d'hyène. *op. cit.*, p. 62.

7. horrible Eternel, à la figure de vipère. *op. cit.*, p. 81.

8. Il était étendu sur la route, les habits déchirés. Sa lèvre inférieure pendait comme un câble somnifère; ses dents n'étaient pas lavées, et la poussière se mêlait aux ondes blondes de ses cheveux . . . Des flots de vin remplissaient les ornières, creusées par les soubresauts nerveux de ses épaules. L'abrutissement, à groin de porc, le couvrait de ses ailes protectrices, et lui jetait un regard amoureux. *op. cit.*, p. 144.

Nine The Language of Dream

1. En effet, j'arrache le masque à sa figure traîtresse et pleine de boue, et je fais tomber un à un . . . les mensonges sublimes avec lesquels il se trompe lui-même . . . C'est pourquoi le héros que je mets en scène s'est attiré une haine irréconciliable, en attaquant l'humanité, qui se croyait invulnérable, par le brèche d'absurdes tirades philanthropiques; elles sont entassées, comme des grains de sable, dans ses livres . . . Il ne suffit pas de sculpter la statue de la bonté sur le fronton des parchemins que contiennent les bibliothèques. O être humain! te voilà, maintenant, nu comme un ver, en présence de mon glaive de diamant! *Oeuvres*, pp. 79–80.

2. une guerre affreuse menaçait de planter son harpon sur la poitrine de deux pays ennemis. *op. cit.*, p. 132.

3. l'homme, ce singe sublime, a déjà percé ma poitrine de sa lance de porphyre. *op. cit.*, p. 159.

4. tu portes, dans ma conscience, ton scalpel qui ricane. *op. cit.*, p. 115.

5. plonger, dans les viscères de l'homme, un poignard aigu qui restera à jamais enfoncé dans son corps. *op. cit.*, p. 108.

6. le triple dard que la nature me donna comme une langue. *op. cit.*, p. 83.

7. sa figure de platine. *op. cit.*, p. 209.

8. L'homme aux lèvres de bronze. *op. cit.*, p. 241.

9. L'homme aux lèvres de soufre. *op. cit.*, p. 248.

10. L'homme aux lèvres de jaspe. *op. cit.*, p. 241.

11. L'homme à la prunelle de jaspe. *op. cit.*, p. 124.

12. L'homme aux lèvres de saphir. *op. cit.*, p. 243.

13. ta cruelle tunique de saphir. *op. cit.*, p. 114.

14. Si la terre était couverte de poux . . . Quel spectacle! Moi, avec des ailes d'ange, immobile dans les airs, pour le contempler. *op. cit.*, p. 104.

15. tu auras fait le mal à un être humain, et tu seras aimé du même être: c'est le bonheur le plus grand que l'on puisse concevoir. *op. cit.*, p. 51.

16. Je parerai mon corps de guirlandes embaumées, pour cet holocauste expiatoire. *loc. cit.*

17. enferme-moi toute la vie dans une prison obscure, avec des scorpions pour campagnons de ma captivité, ou arrache-moi un œil jusqu'à ce qu'il tombe à terre. *op. cit.*, p. 84.

18. Mes pieds étaient paralysés; aucun mouvement ne venait trahir la vérité de cette immobilité forcée. Au milieu d'efforts surnaturels, pour continuer mon chemin, ce fut alors que je me réveillai, et que je sentis que je redevenais homme. *op. cit.*, p. 177.

19. Je suis sale. Les poux me rongent. Les pourceaux, quand ils me regardent, vomissent. Les croûtes et les escarres de la lèpre ont écaillé ma peau, couverte de pus jaunâtre. Je ne connais pas l'eau des fleuves, ni la rosée des nuages. Sur ma nuque, comme sur un fumier, pousse un énorme champignon. Assis sur un meuble informe, je n'ai pas bougé mes membres depuis quatre siècles. Mes pieds ont pris racine dans le sol et composent, jusqu'à mon ventre, une sorte de végétation vivace, remplie d'ignobles parasites, qui ne dérive pas encore de la plante, et qui n'est plus de la chair. Cependant mon cœur bat. Mais comment battrait-il, si la pourriture et les exhalaisons de mon cadavre (je n'ose pas dire corps) ne le nourrissaient abondamment? Sous mon aisselle gauche, une famille de crapauds a pris résidence, et, quand l'un d'eux remue, il me fait des chatouilles. Prenez garde qu'il ne s'en échappe un, et ne vienne gratter, avec sa bouche, le dedans de votre oreille: il serait ensuite capable d'entrer dans votre cerveau. Sous mon aisselle droite, il y a un caméléon qui leur fait une chasse perpétuelle, afin de ne pas mourir de faim: il faut que chacun vive. Mais, quand un parti déjoue complètement les ruses de l'autre, ils ne trouvent rien de mieux que de ne pas se gêner, et sucent la graisse délicate qui couvre mes côtes: j'y suis habitué. Une vipère méchante a dévoré ma verge et a pris sa place: elle m'a rendu eunuque, cette infâme. Oh! si j'avais pu me défendre avec mes bras paralysés; mais, je crois plutôt qu'ils se sont changés en bûches. Quoi qu'il en soit, il importe de constater que le sang ne vient plus y promener sa rougeur. Deux petits hérissons, qui ne croissent plus, ont jeté à un chien, qui n'a pas refusé, l'intérieur de mes testicules: l'épiderme, soigneusement lavé, ils ont logé dedans. L'anus a été intercepté par un crabe; encouragé par mon inertie, il garde l'entrée avec ses pinces, et me fait beaucoup de mal! Deux méduses ont franchi les mers, immédiatement alléchées par un espoir qui ne fut pas trompé. Elles ont regardé avec attention les deux parties charnues qui forment le derrière humain, et, se cramponnant à leur galbe convexe, elles les ont tellement écrasées par une pression constante, que les deux morceaux de chair ont disparu, tandis qu'il est resté deux monstres, sortis du royaume de la viscosité, égaux par la couleur, la forme et la férocité. Ne parlez pas de ma colonne vertébrale, puisque c'est un glaive. *op. cit.*, pp. 169–70.

20. Chaque nuit, à l'heure où le sommeil est parvenu à son plus grand degré d'intensité, une vieille araignée de la grande espèce sort lentement sa tête d'un trou placé sur le sol, à l'une des intersections des angles de la chambre. Elle écoute attentivement si quelque bruissement remue encore ses mandibules dans l'atmosphère. Vu sa conformation d'insecte, elle ne peut pas faire moins, si elle prétend augmenter de brillantes personnifications les trésors de la littérature, que d'attribuer des mandibules au bruissement. Quand elle s'est assurée que le silence règne aux alentours, elle retire successivement, des profondeurs de son nid, sans le secours de la méditation, les diverses parties de son corps, et s'avance à pas comptés vers ma couche. Chose remarquable! moi qui fais reculer le sommeil et les cauchemars, je

me sens paralysé dans la totalité de mon corps, quand elle grimpe le long des pieds d'ébène de mon lit de satin. Elle m'étreint la gorge avec les pattes, et me suce le sang avec son ventre. Tout simplement! Combien de litres d'une liqueur pourprée, dont vous n'ignorez pas le nom, n'a-t-elle pas bus. *op. cit.*, pp. 210–1.

21. l'araignée avait ouvert son ventre, d'où s'étaient élancés deux adolescents, à la robe bleue, chacun un glaive flamboyant à la main, et qui avaient pris place aux côtés du lit, comme pour garder désormais le sanctuaire du sommeil. *op. cit.*, p. 213.

22. il valait mieux se soumettre à ce décret irrévocable. *op. cit.*, p. 217.

23. le crépuscule du matin vienne apporter, par le changement de décors, un dérisoire soulagement à son coeur bouleversé. *op. cit.*, p. 218.

24. Je me tiendrai toujours sur mes gardes, en ayant l'œil sur lui! *op. cit.*, p. 127.

25. c'était une nuit d'hiver. Pendant que la bise sifflait dans les sapins, le Créateur ouvrit sa porte au milieu des ténèbres et fit entrer un pédéraste. *op. cit.*, p. 206.

Ten   The Pattern of Les Chants

1. R. Roussel, *Comment j'ai écrit certains de mes livres* (Paris 1963 ed.), p. 23.

2. La générosité jouit des félicités d'autrui, comme si elle en était responsable. *Oeuvres*, p. 291.

3. Essaie donc . . . de transporter dans ton imagination les diverses modifications de ma raison cadavérique. *op. cit.*, p. 189.

4. j'étais encore à une grande distance du lieu de la scène; car, de même que les stercoraires, oiseaux inquiets comme s'ils étaient toujours affamés, se plaisent dans les mers qui baignent les deux pôles, et n'avancent qu'accidentellement dans les zones tempérées, ainsi je n'étais pas tranquille. *op. cit.*, p. 191.

5. O poulpe, au regard de soie! toi, dont l'âme est inséparable de la mienne; toi, le plus beau des habitants du globe terrestre, et qui commandes à un sérail de quatre cents ventouses; toi, en qui siègent . . . *op. cit.*, p. 56.

6. O pou vénérable, toi dont le corps est dépourvu d'élytres. *op. cit.*, p. 74.

7. En comptant l'acarus sarcopte qui produit la gale, tu auras deux amis! *op. cit.*, p. 78.

Eleven   The Build to Climax

1. L'ange du sommeil, lui-même, mortellement atteint au front d'une pierre inconnue. *Oeuvres*, p. 126.

2. 'Mon père était un charpentier de la rue de la Verrerie . . . Que la mort des trois Marguerite retombe sur sa tête, et que le bec du canari lui ronge éternellement l'axe du bulbe oculaire! Il avait contracté l'habitude de s'enivrer; dans ces moments-là, quand il revenait à la maison, après avoir couru les comptoirs des cabarets, sa fureur devenait presque incommensurable, et il frappait indistinctement les objets qui se présentaient à sa vue. Mais, bientôt, devant les reproches de ses amis, il se corrigea complètement, et devint d'une humeur taciturne. Personne ne pouvait l'approcher, pas même notre mère. Il conservait un secret ressentiment contre l'idée du devoir qui l'empêchait de se conduire: à sa guise. J'avais acheté un serin pour mes trois sœurs; c'était pour mes trois sœurs que j'avais acheté un serin. Elles l'avaient enfermé dans une cage, au-dessus de la porte, et les passants s'arrêtaient, chaque fois, pour écouter les chants de l'oiseau, admirer sa

grâce fugitive et étudier ses formes savantes. Plus d'une fois mon père avait donné l'ordre de faire disparaître la cage et son contenu, cor il se figurait que le serin se moquait de sa personne, en lui jetant le bouquet des cavatines aériennes de son talent de vocaliste. Il alla détacher la cage du clou, et glissa de la chaise, aveuglé par la colère. Une légère excoriation au genou fut la trophée de son entreprise. Après être resté quelques secondes à presser la partie gonflée avec un copeau, il rabaissa son pantalon, les sourcils froncés, prit mieux ses précautions, mit la cage sous son bras et se dirigea vers le fond de son atelier. Là, malgré les cris et les supplications de sa famille (nous tenions beaucoup à cet oiseau, qui était, pour nous, comme le génie de la maison) il écrasa de ses talons ferrés la boîte d'osier pendant qu'une varlope, tournoyant autour de sa tête, tenait à distance les assistants. Le hasard fit que le serin ne mourut pas sur le coup; ce flocon de plumes vivait encore, malgré la maculation sanguine. Le charpentier s'éloigna, et referma la porte avec bruit. Ma mère et moi, nous nous efforçâmes de retenir la vie de l'oiseau, prête à s'échapper; il atteignait à safin, et le mouvement de ses ailes ne s'offrait plus à la vue, que comme le miroir de la suprême convulsion d'agonie. Pendant ce temps, les trois Marguerite, quand elles s'aperçurent que tout espoir allait être perdu, se prirent par la main, d'un commun accord, et la chaîne vivante alla s'accroupir, après avoir repoussé à quelques pas un baril de graisse, derrière l'escalier à côté du chenil de notre chienne. Ma mère ne discontinuait pas sa tâche, et tenait le serin entre ses doigts, pour le réchauffer de son haleine. Moi, je courais éperdu par toutes les chambres, me cognant aux meubles et aux instruments. De temps à autre, une de mes sœurs montrait sa tête devant le bas de l'escalier pour se renseigner sur le sort du malheureux oiseau, et la retirait avec tristesse. La chienne était sortie de son chenil, et, comme si elle avait compris l'étendue de notre perte, elle léchait avec la langue de la stérile consolation la robe des trois Marguerite. La serin n'avait plus que quelques instants à vivre. Une de mes sœurs, à son tour (c'était la plus jeune) présenta sa tête dans la pénombre formée par la raréfaction de lumière. Elle vit ma mère pâlir, et l'oiseau, après avoir, pendant un éclair, relevé le cou, par la dernière manifestation de son système nerveux, retomber entre ses doigts, inerte à jamais. Elle annonça la nouvelle à ses sœurs. Elles ne firent entendre le bruissement d'aucune plainte, d'aucun murmure. Le silence régnait dans l'atelier. L'on ne distinguait que le craquement saccadé des fragments de la cage qui, en vertu de l'élasticité du bois, reprenaient en partie la position primordiale de leur construction. Les trois Marguerite ne laissaient écouler aucune larme, et leur visage ne perdait point sa fraîcheur pourprée; non . . . elles restaient seulement immobiles. Elles se traînèrent jusqu'à l'intérieur du chenil, et s'étendirent sur la paille, l'une à côté de l'autre; pendant que la chienne, témoin passif de leur manœuvre, les regardait faire avec étonnement. A plusieurs reprises, ma mère les appela; elles ne rendirent le son d'aucune réponse. Fatiguées par les émotions précédentes, elles dormaient, probablement! Elle fouilla tous les coins de la maison sans les apercevoir. Elle suivit la chienne, qui la tirait par la robe, vers le chenil. Cette femme s'abaissa et plaça sa tête à l'entrée. Le spectacle dont elle eut la possibilité d'être témoin, mises à part les exagérations malsaines de la peur maternelle, ne pouvait être que navrant, d'après les calculs de mon esprit. J'allumai une chandelle et la lui présentai; de cette manière, aucun détail ne lui échappa. Elle ramena sa tête, couverte de brins de paille, de la tombe prématurée, et me dit: "Les trois Marguerite sont mortes." Comme nous ne pouvions les sortir de cet endroit, car, retenez bien ceci, elles étaient

Notes

d'un cœur fermé à toutes les confidences, et chargé du pesant fardeau d'un secret éternel. Fatigué de la vie, et honteux de marcher parmi des êtres qui ne lui ressemblent pas, le désespoir a gagné son âme, et il s'en va seul, comme le mendiant de la vallée. *op. cit.*, p. 93.

18. votre prostitution, s'offrant au premier venu, exerce la logique des penseurs les plus profonds, tandis que votre sensibilité exagérée comble la mesure de la stupéfaction de la femme elle-même. *op. cit.*, p. 202.

19. Deux piliers, qu'il n'était pas difficile et encore moins impossible de prendre pour des baobabs, s'apercevaient dans la vallée, plus grands que deux épingles. En effet, c'étaient deux tours énormes. Et, quoique deux baobabs, au premier coup d'œil, ne ressemblent pas à deux épingles, ni même à deux tours, cependant, en employant habilement les ficelles de la prudence, on peut affirmer, sans crainte d'avoir tort (car, si cette affirmation était accompagnée d'une seule parcelle de crainte, ce ne serait plus une affirmation; quoiqu'un même nom exprime ces deux phénomènes de l'âme qui présentent des caractères assez tranchés pour ne pas être confondus légèrement) qu'un baobab ne diffère pas tellement d'un pilier, que la comparaison soit défendue entre ces formes architecturales . . . ou géométriques . . . ou l'une et l'autre . . . ou ni l'une ni l'autre . . . ou plutôt formes élevées et massives. Je viens de trouver, je n'ai pas la prétention de dire le contraire, les épithètes propres aux substantifs pilier et baobab. *op. cit.*, p. 159.

20. A. Artaud, *The Theatre of Cruelty*, pp. 51–2.

21. si je laisse mes vices transpirer dans ces pages, on ne croira que mieux aux vertus que j'y fais resplendir. *Oeuvres*, p. 163.

22. Je remplace la mélancolie par le courage, le doute par la certitude, le désespoir par l'espoir, la méchanceté par le bien, les plaintes par le devoir, le scepticisme par la foi, les sophismes par la froideur du calme et l'orgueil par la modestie. *op. cit.*, p. 257.

23. Peut-être que, lorsque j'avance cela, je me trompe; mais, peut-être qu'aussi je dis vrai. *op. cit.*, p. 157.

24. Mes années ne sont pas nombreuses, et, cependant, je sens déjà que la bonté n'est qu'un assemblage de syllabes sonores. *op. cit.*, p. 115.

25. Wittgenstein, *Zettel* (Oxford 1967), I, ii, p. 3 e.

26. un même nom exprime ces deux phénomènes de l'âme qui présentent des caractères assez tranches pour ne pas être confondus légèrement. *Oeuvres*, p. 159.

27. Si j'existe, je ne suis pas un autre. Je n'admets pas en moi cette équivoque pluralité. Je veux résider seul dans mon intime raisonnement. *op. cit.*, p. 197.

28. Vieil océan, tu es le symbole de l'identité: toujours égal à toi-même. . . . tu es modeste. L'homme se vante sans cesse, et pour des minutes. Je te salue vieil océan! *op. cit.*, p. 57.

Fifteen In Conclusion

1. C. Wright Mills, 'Some Effects of Mass Media', in *Mass Media and Mass Man*, ed. A. Casty, pp. 32–3.

2. Il faut lui rendre justice. Il m'a beaucoup crétinisé. *Oeuvres*, p. 247.

3. Comme si cette nichée d'adorables moutards aurait pu comprendre ce que c'était que la rhétorique! Il dit, et, sur un geste de sa main, un des frères se dirige vers la bibliothèque paternelle. *op. cit.*, p. 232.

4. Je les ai vus aussi rougissant, pâlissant de honte pour leur conduite sur cette terre; rarement. *op. cit.,* p. 49.

5. Vous avez reconnu le héros imaginaire. *op. cit.,* p. 225.

6. Rappelons les noms de ces êtres imaginaires, à la nature d'ange, que ma plume . . . a tirés d'un cerveau, *op. cit.,* p. 131.

7. Ce serait bien peu connaître sa profession d'écrivain à sensation, que de ne pas, au moins, mettre en avant, les restrictives interrogations après lesquelles arrive immédiatement la phrase que je suis sur le point de terminer. *op. cit.,* p. 225.

8. cet endroit que ma plume . . . vient de rendre mystérieux. *op. cit.,* p. 224.

9. C'est, généralement parlant, une chose singulière que la tendance attractive qui nous porte à rechercher (pour ensuite les exprimer) les ressemblances et les différences que recèlent, dans leurs naturelles propriétés, les objets les plus opposés entre eux, et quelquefois les moins aptes, en apparence, à se prêter à ce genre de combinaisons sympathiquement curieuses, et qui, ma parole d'honneur, donnent gracieusement au style de l'écrivain, qui se paie cette personnelle satisfaction, l'impossible et inoubliable aspect d'un hibou sérieux jusqu'à l'éternité. *op. cit.,* p. 208.

10. This account of the status of the word in the French language constitutes the central thesis of Professor Ullmann's *Précis de Sémantique Française*. It also plays an important part in his *Semantics. An Introduction to the Science of Meaning*, Chapter IV, 'Transparent and Opaque Words'.

11. son chemin abrupt et sauvage, à travers les marécages désolés de ces pages sombres et pleines de poison. *Oeuvres,* p. 45.

12. sur les ailes de sa pudeur en éveil, et disparaît dans la forêt, *op. cit.,* p. 93.

13. se replonge ensuite dans l'immobilité de son égoïsme, comme une tortue dans sa carapace. *op. cit.,* p. 86.

14. poulpe de la faiblesse de caractère, au requin de l'abjection individuelle, au boa de la morale absente, et au colimaçon monstrueux de l'idiotisme! *op. cit.,* p. 154.

15. les supplices . . . passaient devant mon front en rugissant comme des éléphants écorchés, et rasaient de leurs ailes de feu mes cheveux calcinés. *op. cit.,* p. 99.

16. Je saisis la plume qui va construire le deuxième chant. *op. cit.,* p. 81.

17. êtres imaginaires, à la nature d'ange, que ma plume, pendant le deuxième chant, a tirés d'un cerveau. *op. cit.,* p. 131.

18. pour ne pas m'éloigner davantage du cadre de cette feuille de papier. *op. cit.,* p. 160.

19. j'aurai cependant la force de soulever le porte-plume. *op. cit.,* p. 83.

20. je trouve stupide qu'il soit nécessaire . . . que je place à côté de moi un encrier ouvert, et quelques feuillets de papier non mâché. *op. cit.,* p. 221.

21. Que ne puis-je regarder à travers ces pages séraphiques le visage de celui qui me lit. S'il n'a pas dépassé la puberté, qu'il s'approche. Serre-moi contre toi, et ne crains pas de me faire du mal . . . Davantage. Je sens qu'il est inutile d'insister; l'opacité, remarquable à plus d'un titre, de cette feuille de papier, est un empêchement des plus considérables. *op. cit.,* p. 204.

22. A metalanguage is a convention which permits the linguist to use, say, English as a medium to describe and analyse the peculiar characteristics of the English language, in such a way that his medium is assumed to be free of any linguistic bias that might derive from these characteristics.

Select Bibliography

The Pléiade *Oeuvres Complètes* contains a comprehensive bibliography of Lautréamont studies. However, modern Lautréamont criticism virtually begins with Marcelin Pleynet and Philippe Sollers. Their work was the original inspiration of *Nightmare Culture*.

Lautréamont   *Oeuvres Complètes*—with Germain Nouveau. Editions de la Pléiade (Paris 1970).
Lautréamont   *Oeuvres Complètes* Livres de Poche (Paris 1963).
Lautréamont   *Maldoror* trans. Alexis Lykiard (London 1970).
Lautréamont   *Maldoror* trans. Guy Wernham, together with a translation of *Poésies* (New York 1965).
Bachelard, G.   *Lautréamont* (Paris 1939, new ed. 1956).
Blanchot, M.   *Lautréamont et Sade* (Paris 1949).
Pleynet, M.   *Lautréamont par lui-même* (Paris 1967).
Sollers, P.   *Logiques*, Paris 1968.
Soulier, J-P.   *Lautréamont. Génie ou maladie mentale* (Geneva 1964).
Soupault, P.   *Lautréamont* (Paris 1927).